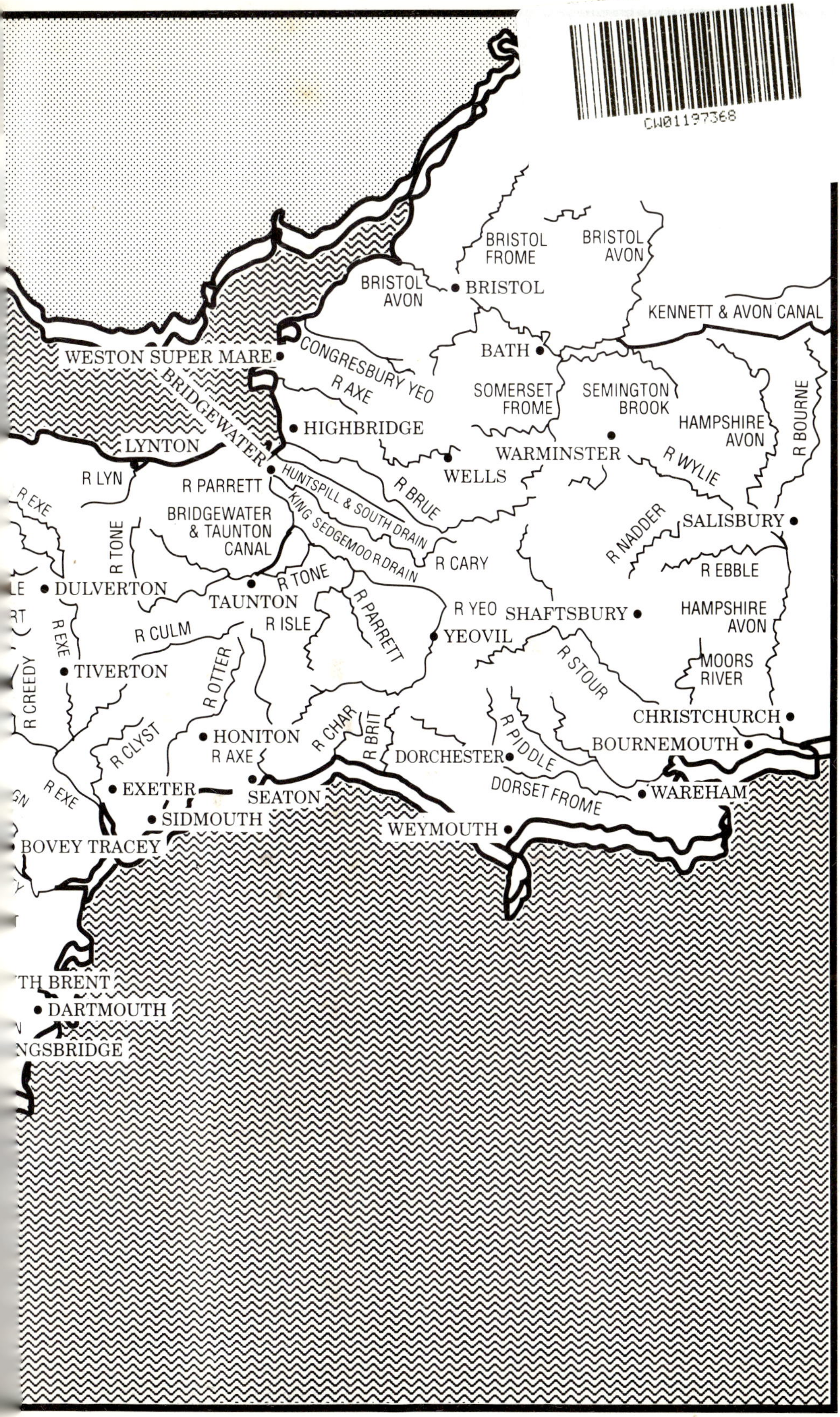
BRISTOL FROME
BRISTOL AVON
BRISTOL AVON
BRISTOL
KENNETT & AVON CANAL
WESTON SUPER MARE
CONGRESBURY YEO
BATH
R AXE
SOMERSET FROME
SEMINGTON BROOK
BRIDGEWATER
HIGHBRIDGE
HAMPSHIRE AVON
R BOURNE
LYNTON
WARMINSTER
R WYLIE
R LYN
R PARRETT
WELLS
R BRUE
R EXE
HUNTSPILL & SOUTH DRAIN
BRIDGEWATER & TAUNTON CANAL
KING SEDGEMOOR DRAIN
R NADDER
SALISBURY
R TONE
R CARY
R EBBLE
DULVERTON
R TONE
TAUNTON
R PARRETT
R YEO
SHAFTSBURY
HAMPSHIRE AVON
R EXE
R CULM
R ISLE
YEOVIL
R CREEDY
TIVERTON
R OTTER
R STOUR
MOORS RIVER
CHRISTCHURCH
R CHAR
R BRIT
R CLYST
HONITON
BOURNEMOUTH
R AXE
DORCHESTER
R PIDDLE
EXETER
SEATON
DORSET FROME
WAREHAM
R EXE
SIDMOUTH
WEYMOUTH
BOVEY TRACEY
DARTMOUTH

A CONCISE GUIDE TO WEST COUNTRY FISHING

A CONCISE GUIDE TO WEST COUNTRY FISHING

MICHAEL SHEPHARD

·THE·
SPORTSMAN'S
PRESS
LONDON

Published by The Sportsman's Press Ltd 1991
© Copyright Michael Shephard 1991

To
Peggy, my wife,
who has good-humouredly endured so much of the
incoming traffic of telephonic inquiries
during the past eleven years when I have operated the
Information Service for the
Devon & Cornwall Federation of Fly Fishers

All rights reserved. No part of this publication may be
reproduced, stored in a retrieval system, or transmitted
in any form or by any means, electronic, mechanical,
photocopying, recording or otherwise, without the prior
permission of the publishers.

British Library Cataloguing in Publication Data
Shephard, Michael
A Concise guide to West Country fishing.
1. England. Fishing (Field sports)
I. Title
799.10942

ISBN 0-948253-48-7

Photoset and printed in Great Britain by
Redwood Press, Melksham, Wiltshire

CONTENTS

List of Plates	vii
Appreciation	ix
Introduction	1
1 The General Picture	5
2 River Game Fishing	11
The Trout – Sea Trout and Salmon	16
3 Game Fishing Rivers	24

   Devon and Cornwall: Exe – Otter – Teign – Dart – Devonshire Avon – Erme – Yealm – Plym – Tamar – Tavy – Lynher – Looe – Seaton – Fowey – Fal – Tresillian – Truro – Kenwyn – Helford – Menalhyl – Gannel – Porth – Valency – Camel – Torridge – Taw – Lyn
   The Cotswolds: Windrush – Coln – Leach
   Sources for River Fishing Permits

4 Fishing for Stillwater Trout	40

   Stillwater Trout – Stillwater Rainbows – Fishing from Boats

5 Stillwaters for Trout	55

   Blagdon Reservoir – Chew Valley Lake – Church Farm – Cameley Lakes – Durleigh Lake – Hawkridge Lake – Sutton Bingham Reservoir – Clatworthy – Otterhead Lakes – Avon Springs – Cranebrook fishery – Hermitage fishings – Flowers Farm Lakes – Viaduct Trout Fishery – Sword Lake – St Algars Farm – Hill Farm Lake – Colliford Lake – Argal Lake – Avon Dam – Burrator – Venford – Meldon – Crowdy – Stithians – Upper Tamar Lake – Wistlandpound – Wimbleball Lake – Kennick – Tottisford – Fernworthy – Siblyback Lake – Drift Lake – Gwarnick Mill Lake – Innis Moor fishery – Altarnun fishery – Crowdy Reservoir – Tinhays Lake – Mill Leat Trout Farm – Newhouse Farm – Venford – Hollies Trout Farm – Gammaton Reservoirs – Blakewell Fisheries – Wistlandpound – Blackmoor Gate – Meldon Reservoir – South Reed Fishers – Roadford – Stafford Moor – Bellbrook Valley – Watercress Farm
   Stillwater Trout Fisheries other than those managed by Water Companies (detailed in Appendix 5)

vi   A CONCISE GUIDE TO WEST COUNTRY FISHING

6   Coarse Fishing and Fisheries   66
    *Bristol Avon Area: River Avon – Bristol Frome – Boyd – By Brook –
    Marden – Semington Brook – Biss – Midford Brook – Chew –
    Somerset Frome. Angling Club Secretaries, Private Lakes, Free
    Fishing with Rod Licence, Disabled Facilities
    Avon and Dorset Area: Avon – Bourne – Nadder – Stour –
    Stillwaters. Angling Club Secretaries and other useful addresses
    Somerset Area: Tone catchment – Parrett & Isle Catchment – Yeo
    Catchment – Brue Catchment – Axe Catchment. Angling
    Associations, Stillwaters Fisheries over Two Acres
    The South West Region: Devon: Barnstaple – Berrynarbor –
    Bideford – Bovey Tracey – Braunton – Chard – Clovelly –
    Cullompton – Dartmouth – Exeter – Halwill – Honiton – Ilfracombe
    – Kenton – Kingsbridge – Newton Abbot – Okehampton –
    Swimbridge – Tiverton – Torrington. Cornwall: Bodmin – Bude –
    Falmouth – Helston/Penzance – Launceston – Liskeard – Newquay –
    Penzance – Perranporth – St Mawes – Saltash – Truro*

7   Bait Fishing for Sea Trout   86
    Upstream Worming

Appendix 1:   Agencies for National Rivers Authority Licences: 95
              South West Region

Appendix 2:   Licence Distributors in Bristol Avon, Somerset   99
              and Avon & Dorset Areas

Appendix 3:   Fishing Seasons.   103

Appendix 4:   National Rivers Authority Rod Licence Duties, 1991   105

Appendix 5:   Fishing Charges for South West Water plc,   106
              Bristol Waterworks Company, Wessex Water plc

Appendix 6:   Peninsula Coarse Fisheries   108

Appendix 7:   Rods – Analysis of Salmon and Trout Catches 1989   111

Appendix 8:   Some Useful Contacts   117

Bibliography and Recommended Reading   118

LIST OF PLATES

1 The author fishing the river Camel below Nanstallon.

2 A small Dartmoor feeder where wild brown trout abound.

3 Dry fly on Widford Pool, river Windrush

4 Blagdon Lake, high summer.

5 Anglers welcome the start of the season at Colliford Lake in Cornwall.

6 A newly-constructed trout lake in the Cotswold hills.

7 A typical deep on a chalk stream, the haunt of large trout.

8 A lack of thigh waders did not deter these youngsters from getting to the fish.

9 Bickleigh Bridge over the river Exe.

10 Innovative fly dresser Michael Veale exchanges feather and tinsel for a piece of bread.

11 Rose Park – a new two-acre fishery.

12 Stalking rising brownies in the shallows of a flooding lake.

13 A well-dressed angler prepared to net a good brownie from Tinhays Lake at Lifton.

14 River Lyn.

15 A 16 lb 9 oz pike caught at 'Claypit' ponds near Bridgwater.

16 Fishing the wet fly downstream.

17 Chew Valley Lake.

LIST OF PLATES

18 Ray Holly from Yate with a 5 lb 4 oz rainbow trout.

19 An angler being rescued from a watery grave in the river Camel.

20 A licensed netsman on the Teign showing the fruits of five hours' labour.

21 Collecting water samples at Burrator Reservoir.

22 Bristol Waterworks' hatchery man spawning a prime brood fish.

23 Roy Buckingham throws a long line to sea trout.

24 Fast-biting rudd demand concentration on a West Country reservoir.

25 Members of Bodmin Anglers' Association at work building a section of a weir.

26 Two limit bags of wild brown trout caught from Colliford Lake.

27 Low water on the Windrush – Asthall Water

28 The Penpont at Altarnun.

29 Chris Lobb of Silverton casting on the Middle Pool at Innis Moor.

30 Eddy Chambers with a 20 lb pike caught at Slapton Ley.

All photographs are by the author unless stated in the captions to the illustrations.

APPRECIATION

In presenting this book to the reader I would like to acknowledge the assistance I have had from many quarters during its preparation and to express my great appreciation of the stalwart contributions made by many individuals and clubs in efforts of varying degree to ensure that those who come later to fish the lovely waters of the West Country will find the same kind of freedom and sport that those of us who arrived earlier were able to enjoy.

It would be impossible to name all who have in one way or another been instrumental in providing the knowledge contained within the following pages, but I wish to recognise a Voice Crying in The Wilderness in the human form of Joe Chappell, who came to the defence of his beloved River Torridge before others took up the cry. Also, my friends among the angling clubs who today contribute more and more to the future of the fisheries they are so fortunate to enjoy.

In particular I would mention Tyson Jackson and the huge example he has set as a riparian owner, Ray Burrows as secretary of Bodmin Anglers Association, whose efforts in making their miles of water more habitable by salmon and sea trout during the past decade won recognition when the club won the Benson & Hedges and Trout & Salmon Conservation Award. Also, David Reinger, one of those 'foreigners' who share our fishing and whose enthusiasm was accompanied in practical form by photographs and information about the Cotswold trout streams, where he is Fisheries Officer of the Cotswold Trout Fishers.

Michael Shephard
Altarnun, Cornwall, March 1991

INTRODUCTION

This book is written for fishermen about fishing, but it does not purport to teach how to fish: it is presupposed that the reader already knows his quarry and how to use rod and line, but is looking for waters where he can apply his skills.

The West Country has welcomed anglers to its rivers since the time when the wild places first became accessible, but those early visitors came in a quest for the wild brown trout that swarmed the spate streams of Devon and Cornwall. Today, sport with rod and line covers a wider canvas and the development of reservoirs during the past decade has introduced a new sport with stillwaters trout as well as another kind of fly-fisherman. Not only that, but stillwaters have brought another opportunity that rarely existed before in the west of the region – well stocked lakes and ponds for coarse fishermen to ply their art!

Together with those established fisheries of Wessex this part of the Kingdom can provide as wide a variety of sport as any other: much of it is excellent, but all of it is not freely available. For this reason the Guide concentrates on what is known to exist and is likely to continue to offer sport to the visitor. Rules and regulations governing fisheries may well alter from time to time and the prices charged certainly will and none of this can be predicted with any accuracy, which makes the role of the fishing licence distributor and the tackle dealer who sells permits (admirably and often one and the same person) the single most valuable source of information about sport in his locality. The days of the tobacconist who issued your licence and was happy to sell you a tuppenny packet of hooks, but understood little of their purpose, are of the past and every main town in the West can boast at least one tackle dealer or licence distributor possessing the latest information about local fishing and a keenness to help the stranger.

To this end a complete list of distributors authorised by the National Rivers Authority (South West and Wessex regions) is published as an appendix, while the addresses of tacklists and secretaries of associations which provide day permits and short-term membership are referred to in chapters reviewing both coarse and game fishing. Also the latest information about angling for trout and coarse fish on reservoirs and lakes controlled by water companies are presented in the appendices, together with addresses of the NRA regional offices and contacts with wardens in respect of the stillwaters fishing of the Bristol, Wessex and South West companies.

It will be readily recognised that the coarse fishing season throughout the Wessex region is that applying to most of England, while no such protection is afforded those fish throughout the South West region or Devonian Peninsula. Again, the fishing season for salmon and trout remains firm in the Wessex region, while it varies considerably from one watershed to another throughout the area of the slightly acidic spate rivers of the far west. These schedules are, in fact, laid out in the appendix as indeed are the returned figures for catches of salmon and migratory trout recorded by rod and line fishermen on these rivers – a pointer to those months of the season that have proved most prolific during recent years. To some extent, however, these figures are affected by the weather prevailing through the months season by season. They do form a useful guide.

This book happily coincides with a growing gleam of hope for the future of the game fishing rivers: for too long, as the wealth of stillwaters fishing of all kinds expanded to fill the vacuum of such opportunity, so had the health of the rivers of west Somerset, Devon and Cornwall declined through the '70s and '80s. The reasons for this decline can be mainly attributed to neglect of spawning grounds, water abstraction, all too efficient drainage, poaching in the headwaters and in the estuaries, illegal use of monofilament nets and, of course, pollution. It is with relief and gratitude that anglers have welcomed not only the promise provided by the formation of the National Rivers Authority, but after some eighteen months of existence the clear evidence that the new guardians of the waterways do have the teeth and have already demonstrated their willingness to use their powers.

The recovery of a sick river takes time, however good the intention of those concerned with its return to health. The cause of the malaise may have been some immediate disaster through the introduction of a noxious element or it may be of an insidious kind that produces a slow but certain decline in water quality, prey foods suitable for the growing young of the fish and, of course, with the passing of years the eventual decimation of whole populations ... just as surely as has been seen to be done over a shorter passage of time by the arrival of ulcerative dermal necrosis or even more immediately by the accidental or negligent (even wilful) discharge of gallons of slurry, silage liquor, industrial acid or even aluminium sulphate into a river. Nature's own flush of acid water into a feeder stream as the result of heavy rainfall after weeks of drought can achieve the same result.

Whatever the cause the recovery of a game fishing river must take time. It cannot be achieved by simple restocking with sizable fish like a stillwaters fishery. In some dire cases not only are fish destroyed, but most of their element as well: the return of clear running healthy water is not in itself sufficient to maintain a stock of fish if there is no food or cover for them. Control of netting at sea or in an estuary is not enough to build up a healthy stock of salmon or sea trout, nor would be the complete cessation of rod fishing if the incoming fish found no gravels clean enough to make their redds and shed the eggs and milt to produce the next generation.

The general reaction of anglers and others concerned with conservation after news of a serious fish 'kill' is to suggest that restocking should be done to make good the loss sustained. True enough, brown trout are being stocked into rivers regularly by fishery owners and to a more limited extent by the NRA, who also raise both sea trout and salmon at their hatcheries, mainly to meet mitigation commitments. It would not be difficult to increase the production of young migratory fish, but those very migrants possess the habit-forming genes of their forebears – the very cause of the salmon's habit of returning to the river of birth at times that vary from one river to another. Ideally, the formation of a bank of young salmonids from all river systems to make good losses caused by disaster at the relevant fishery would make such replacement satisfactory, but it would be a vastly expensive undertaking and the favourite formula for the moment is to let the river and its stocks recover naturally ... back to Nurse Time, the Great Healer. Man's best contribution is to guard the health and security of the maternity wards and the nurseries and police the young fish heading off to sea and the adults coming home from their wanderings in the ocean.

Overall, the NRA is now responsible for all that: but the anglers themselves, whether hotel guests, fishing club members or day ticket holders will be expected to follow the codes of conduct that may exceed the angling limitations imposed by the NRA's bylaws. For this reason, a visitor may find restrictions imposed on the methods of fishing used, the actual baits permitted, the number of fish to be taken in a day or over a longer period.

To this end, also, angling associations are increasingly applying measures to meet situations that can arise at any time. For instance, this is the final year of what has been called the Camel Rehabilitation Plan since that river suffered the serious kill of 60,000 juvenile salmonids three years ago. The plan saw the end to professional licensed netting in the estuary, an increase in the fisheries protection staff and the introduction of two new fish passes to enable incoming sea trout and salmon to reach the higher river to spawn. At the same time the very gravels of the upper river required refurbishing and the manpower for this was provided by the angling clubs of the Camel. Also a River Camel Fisheries Association was formed by riparian owners, clubs and netsmen and among the actions taken to help the recovery of the fish was a six weeks shortening of the season at its beginning (when smolts are on their way to sea), sanctuary areas where rod fishing was suspended and limits to catches. Also most clubs in Cornwall now restrict membership to certain numbers, may reserve certain stretches of river for members only and apply limits to the season when permits will be available to non-members.

The Camel pollution was a *cause célèbre* and the aftermath a good example of what actions may be taken at other fisheries in the future: but it was by no means the first time rod fishermen had been faced with the need to accept controls. The Irish Disease or UDN as it became universally known was an overwhelming disaster that left few rivers untouched: but the gradual decline of fish stocks in the North Devon rivers Taw and Torridge until it seemed that these beautiful streams were approaching death led to severe restrictions on rodsmen by means of a South West Water bye-law limiting fishing methods to 'Fly Only' after April and a catch limit imposed voluntarily by anglers themselves. The two rivers seem to have turned the tide and are on their way back, the recovery now being hastened by a rehabilitation plan in which NRA action is playing a large part.

Another factor leads to some restrictions on the availability of water for both game and coarse fishermen and that is a matter of individual comfort. Angling is to be enjoyed and a day at the waterside can easily be marred if shared by *too* many others. Reasonably enough this has led to limited permits being available at some fisheries, particularly the smaller ones.

In conclusion, while the appendices contain many facts and figures of interest and assistance to anglers, the visitor from far afield may find another source of great assistance in the West Country Tourist Board, whose marketing manager, Mike Weaver, is also a fisherman of skill and in constant touch with fishery matters in the West Country. The Board produces excellent up-to-date handbooks and maps on such things as the widely varied accommodation available to meet all tastes and most pockets. These include hotels, guest houses, inns and farms, self-catering holiday homes, camping and caravan parks in the counties of Avon, Cornwall, Devon, Dorset, Somerset and Wiltshire. And for the family information is available on the many places of interest and entertainment well removed from the piscatorial scene! The West Country Tourist Board is at Trinity House, Southernhay East, Exeter EX1 1QS, tel: 0392 76351.

1
THE GENERAL PICTURE

The West Country today offers the angler the widest possible spectrum of the freshwater sport to be found in the British Isles. From the Cotswold Hills to the toe of the Devonian Peninsula, from the famed Hampshire Avon to all points westwards there is fishing for coarse fish, brown, rainbow and sea trout as well as salmon to be had by the visitor and, on the whole, the cost of it reflects favourably when compared with the price of similar fishing elsewhere.

It was not always so: for many years after the Iron Horse had opened up the West to pioneer spirits and Paddington Station became its gateway, the fish most commonly sought by visiting anglers was the wild brown trout of the streams that run off Exmoor, Dartmoor and Bodmin Moor and, to a lesser degree perhaps, the non-salmonids of the slower rivers that drain the Wetlands of Somerset. The fishing offered in the beginning by now-famous fishing hotels was for brown trout, and rivers that have built up their reputation as sea trout and salmon fisheries since the First World War scarcely knew the fish in those early years. In fact, some angling writers spoke increasingly of their fears that the increasing stocks of *salmo salar* would jeopardise the future of the superb trout fishing they enjoyed on rivers like the Devon Avon, the Somerset Barle and Exe, as well as the Otter and the Axe.

This fishing in wild and remote places where an angler might be almost smothered by the beauty of the countryside and wild life around him was a kind we shall never know again. In relationship to what this part of England had to offer demand was small and the prolific unspoilt rivers could easily supply all that was asked of them. Elsewhere in Britain, of course, the story of the Industrial Revolution was already history, although the ruin it had wrought on the countryside by its pollution was only just becoming recognised.

Such problems missed the West, but the demand for its fishing grew and when the urgent demand for its agricultural products led to a revolution in farming methods and output the rivers began to suffer: not that they had not suffered in earlier days, or at least their stocks of migratory trout and salmon, as the result of damming to provide water power for the mills, unlimited netting and poaching on the spawning grounds.

I would recommend those interested in the background of today's salmon fishing in Devon to read the Poet Laureate Ted Hughes' chapter on Taw and Torridge in *West Country Fly Fishing* – a splendidly sensitive and factual book on all the forms of game fishing these counties have to offer.

Or consider the much earlier survey by W. Earl Hodgson in his *Salmon Fishing*, from which I use a few quotes, 'The Exe salmon fishing has been going from bad to worse...', 'the Otter also is in a bad way and the Fishery Board is defunct', 'the Tamar, largest of the streams in the region, should be an excellent salmon river; but it is not', the 'Lynher, a Cornish stream, was for forty years utterly ruined by pollution from the mines' and 'the Fowey shows a lamentable falling-off...' On the other hand he reports the river Camel in a comparatively good state – rather as the situation appears to be at the time of writing. That was all a long time ago, before our present problems began: but land drainage was already having its effects on the flow of the rivers, populations of the towns were increasing and with that the sewage that found its way untreated to the sea – as indeed it remains a problem now. Reports sent in annually by Fishery Boards to the Ministry were often only a matter of two or three lines of comment, such as, 'Average, trout fishing better than usual ... few smolts to be seen.' In any case they appear to have evinced no interest, let alone comment ... as for action!

However, during the years that followed that turn-of-the-century survey, fishing did improve and by the time proper returns were made of catches by nets and by rods the situation was a great deal more encouraging than it is today: on the other hand angling pressures were negligible compared to now. At the time of the Second World War, for example, a handful of keen young men fished the Cornish streams and individual catches of salmon by one man in successive years soon afterwards were 76 and 68 from the river Camel. In recent years the best score I can name is somewhat more than 20 for salmon, although a few anglers have scored heavily with rewarding totals of sea trout.

An example of the growth of angling interest is in the membership of the Bodmin Anglers Association formed in 1956. That year this club enrolled 69 members and rented some 2^1/$_2$ miles of water, stretches costing from £5 to £10 a year! Four years later the club purchased its first length of Camel for £312 including legal fees, when membership had reached 193. By 1964 this had increased to 300 and a limit of 350 was agreed but three years later this had risen to 400 plus 50 juniors. Today there is a waiting list, but visitors are still able to share the water – about ten miles in all – by way of permits for most of the season. This is, of course, not the only club, but it is a good example of the will of local anglers to keep some fishing for themselves, at the same time having the water to offer others.

As you will see the river clubs provide much of the game fishing available in the western region, while their counterparts in the eastern or Wessex area play a similar role in offering many miles of coarse fishing for visitors to Somerset's streams.

Until comparatively recent times there was little or no coarse fishing available west of the river Exe and only a few private pools containing trout. With the rapid expansion of reservoirs by water companies and the stocking of smaller stillwaters by private owners the picture has changed radically.

Unfortunately, efficient drainage of moors and grazing uplands, water abstraction (especially when the population is bloated by the influx of holidaymakers in the months of high summer), inefficient sewage disposal and pollution from farm and factory continue to have an ongoing deleterious effect on stocks of trout and

1 The author fishing the river Camel below Nanstallon. (*Photo: Peggy Shephard*)

2   A small Dartmoor feeder where wild brown trout abound and can provide fast but taxing sport to the dry fly.

3   A dry fly on Widford Pool, river Windrush. (*Photo: David Reinger*)

4 Blagdon Lake, high summer. (*Photo: Brendon Studio*)

5 With reasonable distance between rods, anglers welcome the start of the season at Colliford Lake in Cornwall.

6 A newly-constructed trout lake in the Cotswold hills . . . feeding time.

7 A typical deep on a chalk stream, the haunt of large trout. (*Photo: David Reinger*)

salmon, whilst the sudden arrival of ulcerative dermal necrosis (so far not blamed on mankind) led to the decimation of salmon stocks and, although not suspected at the time, may have had an even more intense influence on sea trout over a longer period. It was not, of course, confined to the west; but its effects were intense, leading to an end to salmon fishing as we had known it on such popular rivers as the Exe, where at the Carnarvon Arms and Tarr Steps hotels there were no experienced salmon fishermen among the guests when salar put in a return appearance!

The return of the salmon was such as to produce the best annual catches on some rivers since records were first kept; as may be seen in Appendix 7: sea trout did not recover so quickly or so well and the high promise of good runs generally in 1987 and 1988 has not been sustained, anymore than were those at the start of that decade. This may be, in part, due to the drought conditions that reduced the rivers to their bones from spring through to autumn and the successes and failures as season follows season only indicate that what seems to be a great spawning winter can be followed by utter disaster during the early stages of a salmonid's life. And, in the same way, the most exciting departure by thousands of smolts to sea, including those that may have been raised artificially in mitigation, may result only in complete disappointment one or two years later!

As I write, another sea trout season has closed with many hopes dashed once again after another summer of rivers starved of water and the far more serious implications of news from Wales, western Scotland and the west coast of Ireland of a continuing serious decline in the numbers of sea trout returning to home waters. At the moment we just do not know what is going on, nor what the eventual outcome may be. But the coming years may well see the improvements we are all hoping for and some are striving to attain.

Of course, where the stillwaters are concerned – and there are an ever-increasing number of them throughout the West Country – stocking with hand reared trout meets the demand of the fly-fishermen, while the coarse fisheries, both lakes and rivers are self-replenishing and, unless closed to anglers through disease among the fish or the accumulation of potentially toxic blue green algae, are not the same subject for concern.

The bulk of coarse fishing in rivers lies within the jurisdiction of the NRA's Wessex Region. This region was originally divided into three sections by the old water authority and continues so today under the auspices of the NRA.

The Bristol Avon area, bounded by the Cotswolds in the north and the Mendip Hills in the south, contains one of the most important coarse fisheries in the West Country, holding barbel, bream, chub, dace, grayling, perch, pike, tench and trout. Of the latter there is excellent fishing in the upper waters of the river and its tributaries, but the best of this is strictly preserved. South of this is the Somerset area, which can be divided east and west, the latter dominated by hills – part of Exmoor, the Brendons and the Quantocks where the river Tone and tributaries drain the southern slopes, while other brooks and streams run down from the northern part.

In their beginning these small rivers fall sharply and are ideal for trout, of which they are well stocked, but fishing is restricted, although some sections are held by local fishing clubs. The eastern part of the area is in complete contrast, characterised by the Levels through which the rivers Parrett, Isle and Yeo drain the higher slopes to the south and meander to the sea, while the Brue and Cary come from the east and the Axe and Congresbury Yeo the north. Although they have short fast sections suitable for trout, they are mainly suitable for coarse fish and the sluices built to hold back the tides also help to maintain levels in the summer months. As well as these river systems the big drainage channels – King Sedgemoor Drain, West Sedgemoor Drain, New Blind Yeo and Huntspill River – help to provide good coarse fishing and ideal venues for angling competitions.

Finally there is the Avon and Dorset area and in the east of it the famous Avon. The upper river Avon above Salisbury and the tributaries that spread out like fingers in the area of the city are mainly trout streams: below the city the river becomes an important fishery for salmon with coarse fish increasing in numbers to reach a peak at the famous Royalty Fishery at Christchurch. The commercial netting station at Muddiford is a salmon fishery. Its estuary is shared with the river Stour which stems from the heavy soil of the Blackmore Vale: it is quickly affected by rainfall and offers good fishing for large coarse fish, including barbel near its mouth, and has runs of sea trout and salmon into the lower reaches. However, its tributaries Allen and Crane rise from the chalk and hold trout, the Allen being particularly good. Another of the area's rivers to flow from chalk is the Dorset Frome and there is a good trout fishery near Dorchester, where some stocking is carried out, but most of the fish are brownies indigenous to the river. Below the town the river enjoys good runs of large salmon and sea trout. It runs into Poole Harbour, where it is joined by the river Piddle – a trout stream of some note, but, like the Frome, mostly strictly preserved by the riparian owners.

To the east of the region, of course, lie the great trout fisheries of the chalklands – Test, Itchen and Meon – but these are beyond our boundaries. In the north, however, in the Cotswold Hills and outside the Wessex management are rivers I mention now because I knew them and loved them well many years ago. Today they offer very little of their trout fishing to the visitor, but such as there is I have included in the chapter on game fishing rivers. Rising from their limestone beds the rivers Coln, Leach and Windrush run down through the Wold to join the Thames. Unhappily, a situation that was causing concern fifty years ago – water abstraction – has grown progressively worse as the years have passed and, unless there is an end to it or at least some control, may well spell the end to some of the loveliest natural trout fishing in the whole country.

Access to The West

Not very long ago a fishing friend came down from the Midlands and we agreed to meet at a rural pub of our mutual liking. As I approached the village I was a little early for the rendezvous and more than a little surprised to overtake my man, who was walking along a lane, stopping to study the purple moorland through his binoculars. He explained that he had left Coventry at a time he calculated would give him easy motoring to reach our meeting place as agreed. Despite a coffee break to kill time when he realised he was ahead of schedule, he arrived in Cornwall almost an hour earlier than planned – an hour quicker along the route than on his previous visit two years before. By 1991 a motorist driving down from London or similar journeys from the north will cut an hour or maybe two off the time it took him in the 'eighties! He will however be well-advised to arrange for mid-week travel each way at the height of the season, when otherwise the journey may be extended in time by four or five hours.

The obvious feed to the west is by the M5 from Birmingham to Bristol, where the M4 from the London area joins in and there can be traffic chaos. For those who are frightened by, or just dislike driving the motorways, the good old A38 can be a godsend and carry you as far as Taunton and then act as your link with north Devon via the A361. In the same way, if you do not want the M3 and A30 to carry you through the heart of Wessex you can switch to the A303 at Sutton Scotney and enjoy a more leisurely perambulation almost to Honiton. There are numerous variations on this theme to meet your taste wherever you live.

Another route off the mainstream for travellers to mid-Devon and Cornwall who are not pressed for time is the Holiday Route from the M5 at Halberton to Tiverton, Crediton and by the A377 and A3072 through Hatherley, Holsworthy, Bude and the coastal road of north Cornwall; or turn off the A3072 for the A30 at Okehampton and on to Lifton, Launceston and the spinal trunk road through Cornwall. The motorist arriving in the environs of Exeter will have the choice of the A38 to Plymouth or the A30 which is now a trunk road, a dual carriageway for most of its journey to Bodmin and beyond, certainly into the extreme western range of the best fishing!

You can, of course, fly and an increasing number of businessmen do ... to Bristol, Exeter, Plymouth and Newquay, but at the airport you are on your own to make arrangement for onward transmission to your destination. Taxis and car hire is available, public transport is not – a fact that must be considered by those who travel by coach or train.

The public transport service in the West of England is little and not very often, whether to reach your final destination or get to the fishing. The established fishing hotels will undoubtedly arrange to pick up guests from the nearest transport point and see that they manage to reach their beats on the water, but the often remote stretches of river high up in the moors and in the wooded valleys, the reservoirs and lakes are not to be reached without private transport of some sort. The railways that opened up the West to the angler will still get you to the area, but the remote Halts where you descend to meet a waiting trap or cart to carry you and the impedimenta to the welcome awaiting you at pub, farmhouse or cottage are no more and the little branch lines that meandered with the valleys, so often running beside the water to set your pulses of anticipation racing ... they too are of the past. On most public waters available to permit holders by courtesy of association or maybe the Duchy of Cornwall the fisherman will need to organise transport of some sort if he does not have a vehicle of his own. This is often difficult where the young, the old and the disabled are concerned and for those who do not, cannot or are not allowed to drive.

But they are only difficulties that can be overcome and, having got so far, you are sure to manage to attain your goal by the waterside in the end.

2
RIVER GAME FISHING

The Trout

There can be few more idyllic ways of spending a bright, warm day in May than fishing the dry fly along West Country rivers, where the indigenous wild brown trout still thrive in goodly numbers. Dermot Wilson called them the 'little breakfast trout' and it is to those diminutive, free and fast rising brownies that I recommend the fly-fisherman who counts fun and the beauty surrounding him as a greater part of the sport than the day's final count. The recently born reservoir rainbow syndrome has no place on our wild streams!

The small dry fly is, of course, the ideal but there will be days when the surface of the river remains undimpled, when there is no natural hatch or fall of insect to bring the fish to the top of the water and the wet fly may well come into its own; yet there is a between-time – a time when a fly slightly submerged and fished like a dry fly ... upstream ... can prove deadly. This is the time of the Spider and no one has described either the artificial or the method of its use better than the man who first brought it to the notice of the reading angler in his book *The Practical Angler*, first published by A. & C. Black in 1857 ... W. C. Stewart. Of that, more anon.

The brown trout is but a stay-at-home form of *trutta*. I think it is generally accepted that *salmo trutta* is the natural trout of the British Isles, regardless of colour, shape or size, and that to simplify identification the experts have allowed us to use *salmo fario* to distinguish the home-loving fish from the wanderer. Apart from the migratory habit there is little to separate the general behaviour of either from the other during the early days to the time the smolt puts on its silver uniform: then, after its return from the sea, *trutta* works its way upriver to the spawning gravels, just as its brown cousin does in a more limited migration. Because of the rich coastal larders the sea trout grows heavier and faster; because of the change from the depths and subdued light within the ocean it also becomes far more shy in shallow, clear water, but given a coloured river or the cloak of darkness it can throw caution to the winds and seize fly or spinner with a savagery unlike that of the brown trout.

Trutta is a stranger in the river of its birth and infancy: the brownie knows every holt, every bolt-hole within the sphere of its daily task of feeding and usually puts this knowledge to good use as soon as hooked, while that sphere depends on the fish's age and size and its place in the pecking order!

At the risk of generalising I would suggest that on spate rivers where, in any case, food is not really plentiful enough to sustain the prolific breeding local trout to the size associated with the more alkaline rivers to the east, and the seasonal arrival of migratory trout and salmon draws rods to the riverside armed with spinners, flies and worms, it is in the higher reaches that the best brown trout fishing is to be found.

Often the rivers of the West grow from open moorland and often, as the waters swell in their valleys, the banks become heavily bushed and treed and – since security as well as food supply is important to a canny, surviving fish in its choice of feeding place – the best fish usually test the casting ability of the fisherman. Long casting is never needed, while courage and accuracy must impel that wrist action if the fly is to reach, and fall gently before, a fish feeding steadily within the protective arms of willow, alder or the trailing fronds of bankside brambles.

And at the risk of further criticism I will say that casting ability together with that same ability to remain invisible required in the quest for *trutta* is a more reliable key to success than the choice of fly. For many, many years now I have repeatedly heard it said that the number of different flies required to catch the trout of the West is no more than six ... not always the same six patterns by any means, but the principle is the same and some of the newcomers to this list are really only variations on the same theme.

Before we probe more deeply into fly-fishing, let me dismiss other methods because they are dealt with elsewhere. Baits and spinners can be deadly where their use is allowed – especially a tiny Mepp or Devon minnow, even a fly spoon, cast upstream and recovered at a rate greater than that of the current – but the bold little, golden sided and vermilion-spotted *fario* of our small rivers deserve better of the angler, except, perhaps, where a surfeit of all-embracing herbage makes the casting of the fly an impossibility.

In passing, the modern fly-fisherman now has more power to his elbow since monofilament offers him a finer leader point of a greater breaking strain than the old silkworm gut of pre-war days. In other ways nothing much has changed since the turn of the century. There may be fewer trout, but that situation has been improving steadily since the mid-eighties.

That there are more anglers today is beyond doubt: whether they remain through the future years will depend on the fish stocks, but already many of the new rods arriving on the scene have replaced those whose aim it was to end the day with a bulging creel. Fishing hoteliers tell me that many of their guests – especially those from the Continent and America – kill none of the trout they catch, not even those which would make such a delicious breakfast! Although I am not one of the 'catch and release' school and happily confess to some inner glow when I am able to show off a good fish or two, I do only kill those trout which merit admiration of any audience and which I am sure will be a pleasure to eat... either by my family or someone I know will appreciate them.

On this theme I recall asking a Cornish angler of great skills and experience what was the biggest bag of peal he ever made ... back in the good old days, that is. He searched the past and returned with the answer that he had never killed more than ten in an outing. 'Never more than we wanted to eat,' he added, 'sometimes, maybe, I'd give a couple to a neighbour ... even keep one for our cat:

but my mother had no fridge in those days, let alone a deep freeze!' However, there are two sides to that coin and in the days of that old Edinburgh lawyer, Stewart, men made a living and were able to support a family on the hundreds of trout they caught by fly and worm and sold up across the Border; to a lesser degree they did down in the South West, but not many locals bothered to fish as they do today, when also some are prepared to sell their fish. Fortunately, these little fish are beneath their notice and that of the would-be buyers, who have grown accustomed to the size and pink flesh of farm-bred rainbows, the prestige of the silver salmon and the undisputed table superiority of the sea trout.

But conservation never comes amiss and there is much to be said for locating and fishing for the better trout of the river where this can be done, or, where the character of the water makes it impossible, using barbless hooks or at least those with the barb filed. The fish for the freezer syndrome is one of the nastier aspects of the modern stillwaters and has no place where rivers run free and the trout are wild.

Personally, I have no more objection to an angler selling his catch to defray expenses than I have for the shoot that sells game to help pay their way, but I have a rooted antipathy for the 'sporting' fisherman who actually takes the rod out of its bag with the intention of catching as many as maybe in order to make a profit. This was called 'Fishmongering' by a senior member of the old South West Water in 1979 – a term much resented by the reservoir fishing fraternity in the counties of Devon and Cornwall. It did not, in fairness, apply to the majority, but it did to some ... and still does.

So for those who like to sleep sound at night and rise to a handsome breakfast just knock the fish you need on the head *before* it leaves the net or you unhook it and all others release to the water as gently as maybe.

The slightly acidic trout waters of the West Country, rocky but weedless as most are, do not encourage large populations of high protein diets of shrimp and snail and are suited only to those insects whose sub-aquatic forms are able to burrow or find shelter among and under stones. But the large numbers of fish dependent on the river for their livelihood find in spring and high summer an ever-growing abundance of terrestrial foods – caterpillars, beetles, ants, worms and flies – which are blown or washed into the water or fall on it from the lush bankside herbage and overhanging trees. When hungry and on feeding station the trout may find potential foodstuffs come to it on the current in all shapes and sizes and colour. There are occasions when the fish may accept something – say a black gnat or a green caterpillar – to the exclusion of all else and only some emulation of the chosen natural will achieve success for the angler; but in the main, while possibly showing preference for one or another of the morsels brought to it on the stream, the fish will take or inspect anything remotely resembling food!

I proved this on Exmoor's river Barle more than forty years ago and again most recently on the rivers Lynher and Ottery in Cornwall, whilst I enjoyed similar conclusive experiences on many Devon rivers during the intervening years.

During the winter months the river larder is bare and so are the trees and the lank grasses and keksies. Floods may well wash worms downstream, but all in all it is a good thing that Nature has ordained the trout (like peal and salmon when on the run) to lose its appetite and with that its condition. Mature fish will have spawned by Christmas (some of them precociously small in size) and will fall back slowly from the redds to seek the security of the deeper pools out of the force of the current, constrained to save all energy possible until they are able to build up their strength.

So, when the season starts again in the middle of March, well-conditioned trout and good fishing will be in short supply and the wise fisherman will probably leave his rod in its bag or take it to a lake or reservoir in pursuit of over-wintered rainbows – a prize worth having. But if the love is for the river and the recent winter's waiting too much to bear any longer one can fish the river with thought and, possibly, some success. Without any doubt this is the time when the barbless hook must be used: you may catch greedy little parr as well as the tinier trout and you may catch the shining, silvery smolts before they go to sea, none of which you wish any harm. You may also hook thin, dark and flabby brownies – sometimes quite large – if you fish the deeper pools and slack runs. But if you confine yourself to fishing the fly upstream and cast only to the fast water, which at this time only the fitter trout will face, you may enjoy a bit of worthwhile sport and catch a few fish fit to keep for the eating. If, however, you do not want a fish for the pan, do not go fishing until the middle of April at the earliest.

Much depends on the severity or otherwise of the preceding winter and a mild one – like those of 1987/88 and 89/90 – will, despite what some folk prefer to think, bring an early appearance of the natural insect life of spring and an earlier return to full condition in the wasted fish. It is not by chance that Nature uses water temperature to decree the time it takes for the ova of the salmonids to hatch, go through the alevin stage and then join the drama of a river existence as hungry fry!

By April hatches of fly may still appear only thinly, but the emergence of the Dark Olive – *baetis rhodani* – that seems to be well tuned to cold water conditions, will ensure that the trout have something to look up to and that the dry fly-fisherman will see a few rises to fish to, if only for a brief hour or so of the day. At this time of year the Dartmoor rivers will rapidly become a delight to fish and by May the increasing numbers of ephemera – the general family of mayflies as opposed to the large version of which Danica is the type most commonly met with on the slower sections of moorland streams and the broader lowland rivers – can bring wonderful sport and enough brown trout to the net to enable the fisherman to become extremely selective. Few fisheries apply a catch and release rule and whereas size limits apply restrictions of the numbers the angler may kill often do not. It is quite possible to catch a lot of trout in a day, even now, and good to report that very rarely is an angler known to abuse this freedom, whilst many visitors to club or hotel waters retain only a brace or two to enjoy at breakfast next day.

One of the most reliable flies to be fished on Devon streams and the Exe, Barle and Haddeo at this time is the black gnat that appears in May and through June and for a while, the wind direction and strength being right, its larger cousin with the trailing legs, the hawthorn fly, has a chance to make an impact almost as startling as that of the mayfly on the alkaline rivers to the east. Also, with the growth of bankside herbage and bushes and trees, now fully-leafed, a growing army of beetles, spiders, caterpillars, moths, grasshoppers, ants and the like provide variety to the larder. And, unlike their fastidious brothers in the chalk streams, the moorland brownies rarely become snobbish or purist in their feeding. Sometimes they do: then the angler must find out the special dish of the day and imitate it – water bred ephemera, terrestrial beetle or the caterpillars that fall from overhanging branches. It may not occur on anything other than a short stretch of the stream, but the fish can remain very selective during a day, even for a week or two.

Among other insects to make their impact as summer approaches its peak are the pale watery and blue-winged olives and, of course, some of the large family of sedge flies.

Little stocking is carried out on these smaller streams or headwaters of the larger rivers, but the decline in numbers of the native stock and the increased demand for fishing led to fairly comprehensive, but judicious re-stocking on some of the main rivers including the Tamar and its tributaries, the upper Taw and Torridge, Exe, Barle and Haddeo. These all provide excellent dry fly-fishing at times. Personally, I enjoyed some wonderful days on the river Ottery which joins the Tamar near Launceston, one of the main river's water-carriers that boast a mayfly hatch sufficient to interest the bigger trout, but never enough to put them off surface-feeding once it is over. This was during the first years of the 'eighties and it was possible to catch two or three dozen fish during a few hectic hours, fishing fine upstream and with caution. Few of those trout were less than eight inches long and the three best recorded weighed an ounce or so over $1^{1}/_{4}$ lb, although this stretch had not been stocked with many fish or any half that size! Unfortunately, sport faded as the water became tainted with what I always thought to be washings from milking parlours. Today it is happily revived and a good day's fishing can have the added excitement of an occasional skirmish with a sea trout that take quite well in daylight. One season saw fifteen salmon taken from that short stretch but the past drought summers have had their effect and in 1990 there was a serious pollution affecting ten miles of the upper river, the result of which has yet to be seen. In the 'eighties, too, there was a serious slurry pollution on the Carey, another Tamar stream which holds better than average trout but rarely peal and boasts quite a substantial hatch of Mayfly. This was restocked and should not be long in returning to its old self.

Because these trout are accustomed to making the most of the food the river offers your choice of flies can be as catholic as you wish, but more often than not a mere handful of patterns will suffice. Generally, however, they should be tied small – size 14, 16 even 18 hooks – except when the natural insect happens to be a big one.

Moor and valley streams can provide you with great fun to a dry fly but there will be times when conditions or the fish ordain that you will fish wet fly or use the upstream spider: you will still catch fish and it will still be fun.

Once you leave the western moorland or fish rivers that have run far enough from their influence to change character and attain a more sedate status you will find that the average size of the fish increases just as the food supply becomes more regular. Where rivers have good beds of weed showing in clear waters these will be colonised by shrimp and snail and many more of the upwinged flies that will find their order and place through the season, to reach nymphal maturity and rise to the surface to hatch into the gossamer winged insects that return later to the water as the perfect imago to deposit their eggs and die. It is under these conditions that the trout is more likely to conform to a more strictly limited diet and, in the presence of an abundance of like creatures rising to and hatching at the surface or drifting on it, spent after death, will become selective, even choosy in their feeding and require a great deal of finesse of the angler in his casting, the lightness of his tackle and in his choice of artificial fly and its size.

This is a situation which develops even more noticeably as you reach the rivers that spring from chalk and rarely know the sudden fury and darkness of the spate. Such fishing is highly prized and hard to share: its cost to fish is entirely proportionate to this demand and the demand's requirement for heavy stocking with trout of a takable size; brown trout of this kind are expensive and so is fishing for them, compared, say, with the miles of streams on Dartmoor that are available to anyone who purchases a licence and a Duchy of Cornwall permit. It is perhaps the difficulty of finding a place on these richer waters that presents the visitor with only a day or two to spare with the biggest problem.

Sea Trout and Salmon

Some people put the pursuit of *salmo trutta* on a pedestal way above all other forms of piscatorial adventure: others are simply content to welcome those occasions when contact is made – often accidentally – with the trout which comes in from the sea. For many anglers, sport with these superb migratory fish when they arrive fresh from the salt is synonymous with the use of the artificial fly by night; for others the picture is of a spate river clearing as the flood falls – a time when the fish will for a while throw all caution to the winds and seize with violent aggression any lure or spinning bait which comes within the window of its vision. Others seek the sea trout with maggots and worms, employing methods and tackle which vary from the basic use of heavy leads and static bait to the ultimate in the skills of bait fishing – long-trotting worm, maggot, shrimp, sand eel and sometimes such unlikely oddities as cheese or bread down to the fish, manipulating the power and direction of the current to take their offering over some distance of the river or, conversely, casting the bait upstream and allowing the stream to carry it back over the likely lies.

First contact with a fresh-run sea trout is a nerve-wracking experience, usually of short duration, as a series of violent reactions to the hook, including some extraordinary aerobatics, enables the fish to put an abrupt end to its very temporary attachment to the angler. It does seem that the trout newly arrived from the estuary, while showing its readiness to take bait or lure, has a soft mouth which enables it to throw the hook: later, when the mouth appears to have hardened and the reaction of *trutta* to the restraint of rod and line is less sensational, the fish has also lost much of that early readiness to allow itself to become hooked!

Although the behavioural pattern does vary from one river to another, just as conditions of weather and water – indeed of the river itself – will have an effect on the quality of sport enjoyed during a season (from one weekend to another, for that matter), sea trout fishing offered to anglers in the West Country does tend to share a common theme.

All the recognised rivers lie to the west of the Exe. It is not correct to say that this river knows no sea trout: it is, however, true to say that it is not a sea trout river. The total catch by rods in 1987 was 15 fish weighing 29 lb between them! Every other river in Devon and in Cornwall offers a greater or lesser chance of a fish to permit-holders and sea trout or peal, as the smaller school fish are known, do enter even the smallest streams; but these – the Gannel, Menalhyl, Seaton, Tresillian, Erme and Yealm – only provided some 118 fish to anglers in that season.

The table in Appendix 7 shows rod catches for the 1989 season, which was generally a good one: it also depicts the high fishing period common to all rivers in the region – July and August – with the usual June build-up and a tailing off in September, which is the last month of the season for *trutta* and *fario* on the region's rivers. Given the right water and a period of settled weather (which does not often marry happily with the equinoxial storms) this final month can provide some notable sport and a fair number of fish, especially in the higher reaches and tributaries; but the travellers are often losing condition after two or three months in fresh water and a lot of those caught should be and, I am glad to say, are returned. Some fresh arrivals do come into the lower reaches through the month and these include a few of the better fish in the 2 to 3 lb class, succeeding the small harvest peal.

From the start of the season the really big fellows may arrive at any time, but – apart from the occasional stroke of luck – catching them is an art form!

Unlike the salmon the sea trout tends to make repeated annual returns to fresh water to spawn as long as it survives. The splendid $13^{1}/_{2}$-pounder, caught from the river Camel on fly in the early summer of 1988 by Falmouth angler Ken Tebbs, had spent two years in the river before migrating as a smolt, had spawned as a three-year-old and again in the next four seasons and was on its way upriver for the same purpose a sixth time when it fell foul of the rod's size 8 Zulu in a well-known pool on the Bodmin Angling Association's water at the Witching Hour! Fifty-five breathless minutes later it was beached at the tail of the pool, the normal peal net proving too small.

I have known these big fish arrive in the river Fowey as early as March, but – and the time of their appearance in the deeper pools is dependent on water temperature and levels – it is now generally accepted that they will appear in most rivers up and down the country by the end of April and through May. They are no longer gregarious, but numbers build up in the holding pools as successive arrivals come in off the tides. They are shy to the ultimate degree and most likely to be caught on spinner or bait as coloured water fines down following a flood. Or, of course, during the hours of darkness, although the tackle used by most fly-by-nights is scarcely chosen to cope with such powerful adversaries.

Over the years it is probable that more big specimens of the *trutta* tribe than are known have been bagged by anglers and gratefully accepted as salmon without further question. This would most certainly apply to fish caught by day as a salmon in double figures is rarely caught after dark.

Why these big, experienced sea trout should choose to leave the rich feeding of the salt and spend the next five months banting in the often dwindling pools of a summer river makes no more sense to me than the equally odd behaviour of their cousins – the salmon of rivers like the Severn and Wye, or Tweed and Tay. Salmon may come into fresh water in January and endure the snow melt, heavy floods of dirty water, low clear days under a merciless sun when the oxygen supply runs short, the leaf fall ... all this until their purpose is achieved on the spawning grounds a full ten months after they left the ocean!

If this was the habit common to all migratory salmonids I would not question Mother Nature's wisdom: but it is not. Sea trout in the 3 to 4 lb class arrive in West Country rivers in late May to late June, but some fish of similar size do not put in their appearance until September, just before or after the fishing ends and the spawning act is only a matter of weeks away!

On the late season rivers a few salmon may be caught by rods in the first month of the season, in April: but the bulk of the run takes place on the big waters of autumn and winter – salmon finding a fairly easy passage to their redding place through November and December to spawn in January; some even coming into the fresh as late as January and February to drop ova and milt almost immediately, even in March! One warden recounted an experience when electro-fishing a tributary of the Fowey, the St Neot, to pick up salmon for stripping for the hatchery: they captured a kelt ... a cock fish still carrying sea lice on its body. Since these parasites only remain with their host for a short while in fresh water, that fish must have raced up from the sea and mated in a very few days!

We know that the sea trout make as many returns to the breeding grounds as their lives allow and, in view of the short length of most of our West Country rivers and the short time the late salmon spend away from the sea, one might quite reasonably expect *salmo salar* to return to the scene of its birth on more than one occasion. Unfortunately, only a very, very few fish captured have their scales read and our knowledge of their life stories remains unforgivably scant.

Following the arrival of the big sea trout as singletons or in twos and threes the first of the shoals of large previous spawners begin to turn up. These are fish between 3 and 5 lbs and may be accompanied or soon followed by maiden fish returning after a summer and winter of rich feeding. These peal are the exception rather than the rule among the smolts of their year: the majority of the little schoolies, which came back to the river after only two to three months wandering off the coast, may spawn. The very small fish which usually appear back from the estuary from late July through to September (and are often known as harvest peal) probably hang about in fresh water for a while and then return to the estuary to make another run in May, June and July the following year. These little fish, which may weigh less than $1/2$ lb on their return to the river after migrating to the estuary as somewhat backward smolts in late April or May – only a couple of months earlier – will come back the following year as the larger school fish of about $1 1/2$ lb.

This book has not space enough to provide a full analysis of the classes of sea trout which may entertain the sportsman but I hope that this indicates how different groups of fish may be met with as the season proceeds. The consistently successful sea trout fisherman takes one fact into consideration beyond all others: *trutta* is a timorous fish just as it is a bold one!

It is noticeable how trout fry and fingerlings in a hatchery show a much more marked tendency to panic than do those of the salmon – a defensive mechanism which seems to be temporarily abandoned when the fish reach the smolt stage and are about to embark on the great adventure which takes them away from the river of their birth and into the unknown depths and dangers of the salt sea and the rich larder it holds. Salmon and sea trout smolts can be a source of considerable irritation for anglers after the stay-at-home brown trout, throwing all caution to the tumbling waters as they greedily seize flies, spinners and bait.

Whether or not this brief period of madness prior to departure from freshwater is caused by the excitement of a certain change of life, a similar recklessness attends the homing peal as they return to the river and, if the conditions are on the side of the fishermen, big catches can be made without a great deal of care; but this state of affairs does not last for long and the sea trout soon begins to live up to its reputation as 'the fear-fullest of fishes' – a description reserved for the chub by old Izaak Walton, who had never fished for *trutta*.

This nervousness among the shoals of smaller fish is only aggravated by accumulated experience as they grow older, bigger and wiser.

Two conditions assist the angler – one is colour in the water, the other the cloak of darkness: but it is probable that all but the most dedicated of sea trout fishers fail to make the most of the opportunities these allies offer! A fault common to many is that in welcoming the restriction of visibility they forget that fish can 'hear'. Another very limiting mistake is the tendency to believe that fish only live in water across the pool towards the far bank, that the river beneath the angler's feet is only there for wading.

Success with the migratory fish of the West depends on condition of weather and water as much as upon the skill of the fisherman or the methods the state of the river, NRA bye-laws and local rules applied by fishery managers allow. The sport can vary so much with the passing of a weekend, a week or months that the anglers with long-term bookings on beats where demand is great must risk disappointment, no fish, even no fishing at all. But this is a risk taken by visitors to almost any salmon rivers from Tweed to Tavy: in the West, however, the smaller rivers are now so effectively drained that water unfishable at dawn may well produce a fish by dusk; in fact, when I came from Northumberland to Cornwall the speed of the run-off and the rapidity of the clearance of these smaller streams caught me by surprise to such a degree that, having seen the water to be unfishable even with a worm, I did not look again for forty-eight hours, during which time no fewer than fifteen fish were taken from the stretch I wanted to fish.

In the same way the state of the river may suggest that only the use of bait is possible or at best a large spinning lure or spoon: when fishing with only the artificial fly to conserve stocks of fish in Taw and Torridge from the end of April did a growing number of fishermen use flies under conditions unacceptable to them previously ... and discovered that they could still catch salmon.

Except during the first months of the season on the early opening rivers or at the very end of the season on those that close late is the water temperature against the use of a fly – the only lure permitted on the river Tweed at this time, albeit some of those huge and heavy tubes or the method of their presentation bear very little resemblance to fly fishing.

A greater snag is I believe the overgrown state of most of the length of many streams and along certain stretches of most; also the comparatively small size of the holding pools in relation to their depth, which demands the use of a heavy fly, and its skilful use if it is to get down to the salmon quickly enough. This also applies to spinning and accounts for the local preference for Devon minnows up to three inches long and made from heavy materials, although, like the tiny lightly dressed fly in summer, much smaller Devons made of wood will take the fish during times of summer levels, when slower currents flow and the salmon is happier to rise up through the water to intercept.

The past decade or so has seen the return of salmon and sea trout to the rivers after the distressing years of UDN, and with them the fishermen who were not used to local fashions and brought their own assortment of spinning baits or spoons – Mepps, Abu, Toby, Rapalla and the ordinary spoon that has been used by pike fishers since beyond the longest memory. These can be made at home and the copper coloured one is well liked by salmon. However, it is the Mepps that is probably used most commonly by visitors and today by local anglers as well, although the useful medium sizes are sometimes not heavy enough to fish as deep as required and the bigger versions with sufficient weight offer more resistance to the current than one would wish.

However, in the mid-eighties a party of salmon fishers from the Falmouth area of Cornwall visited the river Blackwater in Ireland and heard that French anglers made 'a killing' the previous month using a version of the Mepps that was much heavier and was called Quimperle after the town in Brittany where it was first developed. A French angler also visited the Arundell Arms Hotel to fish the Tamar and David Pilkington, one of the hotel's instructors, was given one and vouched for its efficacy, as, indeed, did the Cornish rods who acquired a few samples during their holiday. By a strange coincidence the town of Quimperle is twinned with Liskeard, the home of the *Cornish Times* in which I write a column on fishing each week. Naturally (although unaware of the twinning) I mentioned this new discovery and that Christmas an envoy from Brittany visited the local town bearing gifts, including a tin box containing half-a-dozen Quimperle spoons from the French tackle dealer!

These were all adaptations to a No 2 Mepps. An elongated lead body gave much more weight to the spoon and was covered by a latex tube body, from which arose the somewhat indelicate nickname of Flying Condom. There was certain difficulty in obtaining a suitable rubber for the covering, but Garry Champion of Falmouth obtained a supply from Norway and manufactured to his own and a limited demand: my doctor discovered that the material used today for catheters is not suitable! Anyway, an Irish firm is marketing a Flying C and these are now available from a limited number of tackle shops.

Whatever the lure you use, its size may need to meet the degree of visibility in the water as well as allowing you to fish it at the required depth. With spoon as with the fly an angler may need to change the size of his offering two or three times during a day on a fast clearing stream following a flood, and the combination of visual quality and weight is far more important than colour or action of the lure. There are times when, as I said, a copper spoon achieves wonders, when on the other hand a Yellow Belly Devon does the trick, while on another it may well be a Blue and Silver, a simple Gold or Silver or some other combination of colours or a Mepps with blue spots on or a Zebra-striped Toby . . . it may be anything, which also applies to flies.

It is truly said that the bait longest in the water catches most fish and that the type of lure most frequently employed does the same, which also can be true: but not necessarily in proportion to the amount of time it is in use compared with less popular models! I had the opportunity to study the day-by-day performance of rods on one famous river and at the end of the season analysed the ghillies' weekly reports. The catch was conveniently 100 salmon, of which no fewer than 76 had been caught on a Garry or Yellow Dog in tube form because we only experienced an autumn run when the river was big. This result came from that fly being used on 90% angling hours but I think it was a Hairy Mary, the fly that caught 14 of the balance, that enjoyed only 6% popularity under summer conditions when both salmon and fishers were present in smaller numbers, while a Blue Charm used during 4% of the total fishing time accounted for 10 fish, as well as a number of big sea trout!

In the final analysis it must be the man with the best knowledge of the water in its many moods and the ability to fish the varying contours and condition of its pools who will catch the fish, be it on fly, spinner, worm, prawn or shrimp.

With another reminder that none of these baits may be permissible on the river of your choice or at the time of the season you choose to fish, it has to be said that a well-presented shrimp or worm, fished free-range or by float, must have the edge over the fly in low water, although the latter will outfish any spoon apart from the tiniest Devon or minute Mepps fished upstream and retrieved rapidly. Personally, on our small rivers I would always select shrimp rather than prawn under clear conditions, while the worm has to be top choice when the river is coloured. A gob of worms fished on a heavy ledger will catch salmon when the fish can only sniff out the bait, but the method is as distasteful as the very name gob!

Visitors to association waters do, of course, find themselves in varying degrees of competition for pools with others – a disadvantage that increases at the height of the season. This includes the static rod fishing the static worm, rather like the goat tethered to draw the tiger, who takes up position on a pool and remains there until the day ends or maybe into darkness. Fortunately, an increasing number of fishing clubs are discouraging pool hogging as well as any unsportsmanlike practices and at this point I wish to stress the fact that the correct use of bait is neither unsportsmanlike or unmannerly; skilfully employed it can be deadly – the reason why some or all baits are barred on certain rivers or at certain times of year.

Even where no holds are barred by bye-law, angling associations do limit their use in certain areas, apply a fly-only night fishing rule on stretches where the fly rod can be used, also limit the time one rod can remain on a pool to, say, twenty minutes. This does not by any means apply to every club water, but the situation does seem to be improving, although it is difficult to prevent congestion on parts of a river at such time as the fish are in, but water conditions limit fishable water to the lower or upper beats only. It happens and the only consolation is that the presence of any number of anglers does suggest that the salmon or sea trout are there!

As with spinning lures, fly patterns vary with the changing moods of anglers and there is a definite danger in relying on any one pattern because it was very successful in the past: there is no good reason for a salmon to take a fly, so there is nothing to imitate. Colour, yes, size, yes, and method of presentation, yes, these are important and it is the wise angler who rings the changes if at first he does not succeed, although for some blind faith and perseverance may be rewarded in the end. This, in my opinion, applies particularly to night fishing for sea trout, when a fly of any size may catch a fish, but sooner or later the trout goes off that pattern. Once again a change in size and or colour may prove useful.

However, the reason the fish stopped taking the offering that proved successful initially might be that one has been pricked by the hook and transmitted its warning to the others: more probably that you have made your presence too clearly evident and have frightened the fish by repeated and heavy casting, by showing your movements against the skyline, by any of a number of seemingly minor awkwardnesses that can be brought about by the smallest of movement after dark. Disturbance of a pool will undoubtedly put the fish off, but they will settle much sooner than many think if left alone. For this reason it is a sound policy, when following another rod on a pool in daylight, to sit and think and watch the water. When salmon fishing I never mind very much if I have to fish the water after another rod, even when I am using a fly and he has covered it with a spinner: with sea trout it is another story and one cannot emphasise often enough the complete need to assume a mantle of invisibility when fishing for such shy quarry by day and remember that darkness itself does not remove the same need for cautious casting, each cast being an individual exercise with the same gentle-

8 A lack of thigh waders did not deter these youngsters from getting to the fish – even in the cold water of early May.

9 Bickleigh Bridge over the river Exe crossed by the road from Exeter to Tiverton. There is fishing to be had here for salmon and wild brown trout from the hotel on the bank, the Fisherman's Cot.

10 Innovative fly dresser Michael Veale, author of *Fishing Flies and their Plumage*, exchanges feather and tinsel for a piece of bread in a light-hearted assault on carp in a private pool ... coffee and biscuits on their way!

11 Rose Park – a new two-acre fishery where the stark banks will be transformed by natural herbage and the small island has been planted with shrubs.

ness and accuracy and high concentration. Frequent casting must cause disturbance and defeat the end.

Further, whether using fly, spoon or bait the need for accuracy of casting is paramount: so often is a grilse or salmon drawn from some recess under the far bank by the lure that falls so close to it as to threaten catching up with the bank or herbage itself, while any less bold approach, averting such dangers though it may, will possibly not be seen by the fish. Sea trout, too, love to tuck themselves away in such hiding places during the daylight hours. The rest of the skill lies with the angler's knowledge of the conformation of the pool and the lies of the fish under varying heights of water – knowledge to be gained by experience, although a good local guide is absolutely invaluable when such rivers are visited for the first time.

3

GAME FISHING RIVERS

As a generalisation the West Country's game fishing rivers – those offering the opportunity to fish for brown trout, sea trout and salmon by way of day permit or short period ticket – are limited to the south western region of the National Rivers Authority and are those of west Somerset, Devonshire and Cornwall. On some the angler may expect to find excellent fishing for brown trout of a size larger than the indigenous or home-bred fish. These are stocked waters and the quality of the fishing is reflected directly by its price. On the other hand many of these rivers, especially in the higher reaches, hold good stocks of the handsome little native fish where the prize may be a half-pounder only, although the sport it provides may well shame a bigger fish.

Almost every river running from the moors into the Bristol or English Channel claims a run of sea trout: even the river Exe which is the one major river said not to hold this claim does produce a few fish every year, while some tiny streams – not big enough to appear on most maps – are hosts to runs of peal that must be reckoned considerable when viewed proportionately. These, however, cannot be included as sea trout fisheries any more than the Exe: but tables in Appendix 7 show the size of rod and net catches over the years, which suggest their importance to the angler. Similar tables show the numbers of fish taken each month through the season and this is the best indication to the visitor when deciding on the time of his holiday or long weekend. When considering any of these figures it must be remembered that the time of arrival and numbers of migratory fish are greatly influenced by the state of the rivers – in other words the weather, which may well affect the month in which a run of sea trout, grilse or salmon can take place: and even the time of the tides with which the incoming shoals may ride from the sea, thus making the choice of one week preferable to the one preceding it!

The size of the trout and salmon likely to be encountered depends partly on the time of year, but more so on the norm for any one river. On some rivers the main run of fish are grilse and on all of them it is grilse that form the bulk of the summer fishing, although a few larger summer salmon filter in and where a late season run occurs some large salmon can be expected – especially on the late closing Cornish streams.

The NRA bye-laws vary slightly from one fishery to another: seasons differ, some methods and baits are taboo here, but allowed there, while local rules applied by riparian owners, fishing hotels and angling clubs may further limit fishing activities. For instance, one drastic limitation applies to fishing on the North Devon rivers Taw and Torridge, where the use of shrimp, prawn, worm and maggot is prohibited and spinning is barred from the end of April. This is because of the serious decline in salmon stocks and it is backed by an appeal to anglers for a voluntary limit on catches and the return of hen fish towards the season's end. Similar restrictions are applied on all permit fishing along the river Camel in Cornwall, where certain stretches are sanctuaries, the start to the official season is curtailed and a limit of two salmon in one day and four sea trout in one day is enforced: further, no angler may take more than four salmon in one week. Such restrictions may, of course, be relaxed in the future if the stock situation improved but equally similar limitations may well be imposed on other rivers.

Sea trout seem to conform to a pattern: large fish arriving singly or in twos and threes as early as March, smaller fish between two and three pounds following in May and June, after which the school peal are expected, their numbers peaking in late July and early August. During a wet summer when rivers are full the trout may move far more quickly than salmon and disappear into the higher beats and feeder streams; in drought conditions, the fish are often disinclined to run, moving up only a few pools on a small rise of water, sometimes falling back again, while the smaller school fish are known to test fresh water and return to the estuary if it is not to their liking. During the past decade and more the sea trout have proved to be entirely unpredictable.

The non-migratory trout are almost entirely brownies, either wild native fish weighing around four or five to the pound or larger fish according to the stocking carried out. In the moorland streams a wild native pounder is a rarity, but they do turn up. Where rainbow trout occur it is certainly due to accidental escapes from fish farms as happened recently and drastically on the river Exe.

River Exe

The main river is formed by the union of the rivers **Barle** and **Little Exe** at Dulverton, joined soon afterwards by the small river **Haddeo** which flows down from Wimbleball Lake. All these streams rise within the Exmoor Forest and offer some fine sport with wild brown trout supplemented by larger fish where these are stocked. When rainfall allows, both Barle and Exe enjoy a fine run of grilse, the first of these possibly arriving in July although drought conditions may defer this until September at the end of which the season for both trout and salmon ends. Fishing is free to residents at the Exmoor Forest Hotel* and day tickets may be obtained on both Exe and Barle, also on a limited length of the river **Bray** at Brayford. At Dulverton an unusual feature is some 500 yards of free fishing for young people under 16, details of which can be had from Lance Nicholson Tackle. Here also is the Carnarvon Arms Hotel, where some five miles of Exe and Barle are reserved for residents. However, non-residents should telephone the previous evening to inquire whether any vacancies exist for the following day. Further up the Barle, on route for Simonsbath, the Tarr Steps Hotel at Hawkridge offers three miles of free fishing to residents and day permits

*Addresses and telephone numbers will be found at the end of this chapter, on pp 37–39.

to non-residents: salmon reach this area on a good water. Below Dulverton at Exebridge John Sharpe can provide fishing on the Exe and Haddeo, also on a small lake stocked with rainbow trout. The trout in his beats are both wild natives and stock fish. From this point the main river continues to Tiverton, where it is joined by the river **Lowman**. In the town the public river walk provides half-a-mile of fishing for trout and salmon by day or season ticket to the general public (with free permits for NRA licence holders under 16): contact M. J. Ford at Country Sports, Tiverton. He can also advise on some $3^1/_2$ miles of water offering brown trout and grayling fishing, but only to those residing within the Borough. Downstream the Fisherman's Cot Hotel has a limited stretch of water along the banks of its land at Bickleigh Bridge and provides permits for the casual visitor, also offering accomodation. There is a good salmon hold here, but the beat is limited.

From this point the river is usually able to hold salmon from the beginning of the season and a few miles downriver the **Culm** joins it from the east and a little further towards Exeter the river **Creedy** flows in from the west and below the city the river **Clyst** joins the Exe estuary. The Crediton Fly Fishing Club has water on the main river, Creedy and river **Yeo** and visitors may use members permits by personal arrangement. This fishing is for brown trout, which applies also to the river Culm at Hemyock where four miles of fishing is available by season, weekly and day tickets obtainable from The Bakery, Hemyock, by postal inquiries. Salmon fishing can be had also on the Creedy and Exe by limited season and day permits from Exeter Angling Centre; day permits also from Topp Tackle, Taunton and Country Sports, Tiverton. Salmon are usually in the lower river from early spring and, given the water to run on and an equable temperature can reach the top waters very quickly indeed.

River Otter
East of the Exe the river **Otter** stems from the little Otterhead Lakes of Wessex Water and runs down by Honiton and Ottery St Mary to join the sea at Buddleigh Salterton. This has long been a classical trout stream, beloved by generations of fly fishers and, although beset by a host of problems today, will be restored to full health before long. It is a delightful stream to fish. Occasional salmon and a few sea trout enter the river but it remains primarily a brown trout stream with six miles of bank and one mile on the **Coly** tributary available to residents at the Deer Park Hotel, near Honiton and day permits can also be had by non-residents. Fishing on a very small stretch at Weston is free to NRA licence holders by arrangement with the owner of the Otter Inn. Free fishing is also allowed to licence-holders by the Clinton Devon Estates along $1^1/_2$ miles of footpath by the river between Clamour Bridge and White Bridge near Budleigh Salterton.

River Teign
The **Teign** rises on the high moor west of Chagford, one tributary coming from Fernworthy reservoir and close to the cradle of the river **Bovey** which joins its neighbour between Bovey Tracey and Newton Abbot, whence a long estuary

carries their waters to the sea at Teignmouth. Suffering like all Western rivers over the past few years from lack of water the Teign can be a good salmon river and offers some of the best sea trout fishing to be had in the country. Most of its fishing is available to the visitor through the upper and lower river associations. Trout are plentiful, but the fishing clubs do impose restrictions on salmon and sea trout fishing to visitors on some parts of their waters. Twelve miles of the upper river is available by permits from the Upper Teign association. Permits are obtainable from The Angler's Rest at Fingle Bridge, Bowden's in Chagford, Drum Sports in Newton Abbot, the Mill and Hotel, Sandypark, Clifford Bridge Caravan Park and the Angling Centre in Exeter. At Dunsford fishing on some $^{3}/_{4}$ mile single bank is available from Steps Bridge Hotel. Then approximately 18 miles of fishing is available to a limited number of rods on the Lower Teign Fishing Association fishery: tickets can be had from Drum Sports.

River Dart
Another of the southern running rivers rising from Dartmoor is the **Dart**, its two initial branches, the East and West Dart joining forces at Dartmeet Bridge near Hexworthy. This river probably offers more opportunity to visiting trout fishermen than any other in the West Country. Many miles of its delightful moorland route are the property of the Duchy of Cornwall and these are open to anglers in possession of the NRA licence and prepared to pay the very modest charges levied by the Duchy. The trout fishing here is well-described by Mike Weaver in that happy gathering of writers on angling in Anne Voss-Bark's *West Country Fly Fishing*. From the Blackbrook tributary of the west Dart and the Cherry Brook at the head of the eastern branch the river Dart provides some dry fly fishing to be described at times as exceptional. To make a good bag of worthwhile trout requires much experience of the river in its different seasons but the real tyro can hope to catch a few fish on his or her first visit providing they combine fieldcraft with the selection of fine leaders, small dry flies or those that fish just below the surface – spiders and nymphs.

You can accept Princetown and Postbridge as the first of the villages on the west and east branches of the river and licences and permits are available at the Post Offices at each. There are many others (listed at the end of the chapter) which can also provide information about other waters on the Dart where sport with salmon, sea trout and brownies is available. There are limited facilities for sea trout and salmon fishing on other beats controlled by the NRA south west region.

River Avon
This particular **Avon**, the Devonshire Avon, was once thought to be the most prized trout stream west of the Otter: it held primarily wild, native brown trout of a size much larger on average than those living in other Dartmoor waters. It offered the most delightful dry fly fishing in a valley remote from the turmoil of war or the daily drudge of business life and once deposited at Loddiswell station, having made the connection from the Great Western express at South Brent, the

angler was alone with the fish, his thoughts and the abundant wild life of that lovely valley. It has not changed a lot, not the valley – although the railway ceases to connect with the main line any more. The Marble White butterflies are still there at their time, even if the numbers and size of the brown trout have decreased. But that is what we were warned about by the first BB in his book *The Trout Are Rising*, more especially by A. G. Bradley in his book entitled *Clear Waters*.

Published soon after the beginning of the Great War its author referred to so much of the beauty of this valley that I have encountered 75 years later that, surely, it cannot have changed so very much – apart from the fact that the train no longer connects with the express from Paddington and chuffs along the valley past Woodleigh wood ('Udleigh 'ude, in the vernacular)?

The river has, however, altered : no longer are its trout as numerous and to some extent the fears expressed by Bradley may have become in part realised; the run of sea trout has increased, but the Avon cannot be considered anything other than a third class salmon river, if that! Bradley's concern was that some attempt might be made to 'spoil one of the best trout streams in the county' by turning it into a second-class salmon river. That it is no longer the river he knew or the fecund source of brown trout of the mid-nineteenth century is not argued, but the reasons stem from causes other than a marked increase in stocks of peal and, to a lesser extent, those of salmon. It still is a delightful trout stream, almost 15 miles of which are available to the visiting fly fisherman willing to pay for a week, two weeks or a months' sport – no day tickets – by application to the Avon Fishing Association or by obtaining a permit from Loddiswell Post Office or Mr O'Neil of Kingsbridge. I stress that this is fly fishing only, except after October 1 when spinning for salmon is permitted below Silverbridge.

River Erme
The Avon runs down to a long estuary below Aveton Gifford and joins the Channel near Bigbury-on-Sea: a few miles to the west is the estuary of the river **Erme**, one of a nest of small rivers that lie in the high moor between the Avon dam and Burrator reservoir. It has suffered a series of serious pollutions during the past decade, but holds good brownies and enjoys runs of both sea trout and salmon. Unfortunately, there is little fishing to be had by the visitor, whose best bet is to contact the Mill Leat Trout Farm at Ermington.

River Yealm
The next along towards Plymouth is the **Yealm**. Holding trout, sea trout and salmon at the time of writing there is no access to its fishing for anyone other than by permission of the riparian owners.

River Plym
The **Plym** rises close to the sources of the Erme and Yealm and is joined by the river **Meavy** from Burrator reservoir before running on to the sea at Plymstock, only a short distance across part of the Sound from Plymouth. In the past this

otherwise excellent little river, prolific of both late running salmon and the sea trout at its best, has been badly poached. It can only offer limited fishing and at the height of any run is over-fished. Two week-day tickets are available to visitors through D. K. Sports on the Barbican and membership of the Plymouth & District Freshwater Angling Association. Permits are also available to non-members through the Tavy, Walkham & Plym Fishing Club and from the Rock Stores in Yelverton and tacklists in Plymouth and Tavistock.

River Tamar
Like the Exe the **Tamar** is a border river, running right across the Devonian Peninsula from north to south and recognised as the county boundary between Devon and Cornwall for most of its course. Its beginning is where the trout fishery of Upper Tamar and its immediate neighbour the coarse fishing lake of Lower Tamar lie near Kilkhampton, a few miles east of Bude. The upper river's waters are joined progressively by tributaries from both east – **Claw**, **Carey**, then the joint waters of the **Thrushel**, **Wolf** (at the head of which is the big new **Roadford** reservoir) and **Lyd**. From the west comes the water of the rivers **Ottery** and **Inny** and, finally, the main Tamar is joined by the estuary of the river **Tavy** – a force to be considered by itself.

Although the Tamar has been renowned and loved by game fishermen for many years, it was originally so because of its trout: even today, its tributaries contribute much of the sport that can be enjoyed by the visitor as well as to the total catch of fish credited to the main river. The brown trout fishing on Carey and Thrushel, the sea trout of the Lyd provide a large part of the sport that the Arundell Arms Hotel at Lifton can provide its guests: while members and permit holders who fish the waters of Launceston Anglers Association find much of the fishing available on the rivers Kensey, Ottery and Inny. Members also have the opportunity to apply for the limited number of rods and half-rods available on the Bamham Water beats of the Tamar.

The river's higher reaches and its tributary the Claw can be fished for brown trout over $6^1/_2$ miles of banks from West Clawton by permits available from Ray Beare Sports in Bude and from the DIY Centre, Holsworthy. For membership of the Bude Angling Association write to the secretary enclosing 50 pence for maps. Permits for the Launceston club waters can be had from Mike Summers Angling Centre, Launceston who can provide permits and information about a number of fisheries in the area. The next available water is that of the Arundell Arms Hotel and this fishing extends over some twenty miles of Tamar and tributaries including some very useful fishing on the Ottery. A small stretch of the Inny offering salmon and sea trout when the water conditions are right, as well as some brown trout, is open to members of the Liskeard & District Angling Club, details of which appear under the river **Fowey**. Visitor permits are also available.

The next major fishery on the river Tamar is some miles of water, nine in all, let by the week to guests at Ensleigh House Hotel, Milton Abbot on the road to Tavistock from Launceston. This water averages 200 salmon annually for its rods and is divided into five beats, each carrying two rods. Permits are sometimes available to non-residents if a beat is vacant and inquiry should be made to the manager. After April these beats are fly only, except for one.

River Tavy
Although it shares an estuary with the Tamar the **Tavy** is a fishery in its own right, sometimes attaining excellence, and the sport it offers can be shared by visitors by way of season, week and day permits obtainable from tackle shops in Tavistock and Plymouth, also the Rock Stores in Yelverton. This also applies to its tributaries Walkham and Meavy as well as the Plym and for membership of the Tavy, Walkham & Plym Fishing Club contact the secretary.

We leave Devonshire to consider the major and important streams in Cornwall before reviewing the northward flowing rivers of both these counties and Somerset.

River Lynher
This river is one of the few where sport with salmon and sea trout has been on the upgrade through recent years: one hundred years ago, polluted to virtual extinction by wastes from the mines, the **Lynher** had been virtually fishless for 40 years. Today, although the runs fluctuate quite drastically from season to season the river provides quite good fishing for brown trout in its higher reaches, sea trout through most of its length and salmon, which can arrive in the lower beats on the edge of the tide before the season starts. In fact, although it rises close to the eastern edge of Bodmin Moor, near the village of Trewint on the A30 and not far from the sources of rivers Fowey and Inny, the Lynher as a game fishing river shares more in common with its Devon counterparts than its Cornish neighbours. Permits are available to visitors through the season, details of outlets for these are given under River Fowey and maps are available showing the beats and stretches of rivers under the control of Liskeard & District Angling Club, which give access to some 30 miles of fishing.

Rivers Looe & Seaton
These small streams are next westwards along the coast and fishing can be had by permits issued on behalf of Liskeard & District AC as shown under River Fowey. Both hold wild brown trout and have small runs of sea trout and the occasional salmon.

River Fowey
With its northern neighbour the river Camel the **Fowey** is at the present accepted as the best of the purely Cornish rivers for salmon and sea trout (with the reservations expressed in my Introduction). It rises high on Bodmin's eastern moor and passes beneath the new A30 motor road just east of the hamlet of Bolventor, where the Jamaica Inn is today one of the best-known landmarks in the county. For more than ten miles the Fowey remains a small stream running through marshy bottoms below the bastion of the moor and is a clear, bright stream full of luxuriant weed: a splendid spawning area and nursery for the sea

trout and now for salmon, since the water authority has made Golitha Falls passable for the bigger fish. Like the little De Lank, a feeder of the Camel that rises close to it, the little Fowey bears scant resemblance to a spate river until reaching the Falls.

Close to Golitha the river almost touches the A38 at Doublebois Bridge, west of Liskeard and runs between the road and the main railway line, perched high up on the wooded hills, to Bodmin Parkway station, where the river leaves the roadside, passes beneath the railway viaduct and heads south for the head of its estuary at Lostwithiel and the sea at Fowey. From the moorland it skirts the main river and gets water from several small streams, its major supply coming down the St Neot river, which now carries a more regular and heavier volume of compensatory water from Colliford Reservoir. This new source has coincided with several seasons of indifferent sport and many fishermen are blaming the quality of the release for this. As the result of investigations carried out by specialists in the field and the existence of other factors currently affecting sea trout and salmon runs on many others of our rivers as well as those in Ireland it is as yet too early to assess the situation accurately and, knowing the ways and uncertainties of the sea trout, coming seasons may well see a complete reversal of the gloomy facts and figures facing us at the moment.

Liskeard & District AC membership has been limited, while visitor's permits are only available on club waters up to October 15: however, since the Fowey and Camel seasons continue for a further two months, the local club's water ends at Bodmin Parkway, where Bodmin Anglers have a short stretch, after which a nice piece of water runs down below the estate of Lanhydrock House and is owned by the National Trust, from whom season and day permits can be obtained for two miles of fishing by writing to the secretary of the Lanhydrock Angling Association. Rods are limited and early application is strongly advised, as is any application for membership of any game fishing club in the South West.

The bottom of the Lanhydrock fishery is the beginning of another very interesting piece of the Fowey. This is the Restormel stretch, running as it does below the ruins of Restormel Castle until it reaches tidal water at Lostwithiel bridge and holders of the current NRA licence can obtain a Lostwithiel Fishing Association card from the treasurer, the Angling Centre in St Austell, Fourways Autos of Lostwithiel or the Bodmin Trading Co. Incidentally, fishing in the tidal water through Lostwithiel Park is free, but anglers must possess the NRA licence: there is also a short stretch of free water on the river's left bank downstream of Respryn Bridge, below Lanhydrock Park.

Another useful piece of water, especially for sea trout, is the Rivermead reach above New Bridge and the Parkway station. Holiday chalets are available here and inquiry should be made to Rivermead Farm.

The Liskeard Angling Club with substantial water on the river Camel, Lynher and smaller streams, has a waiting list for its membership, details of which may be had from the club's secretary or treasurer. Permits are available at a number of other sources as listed on p. 38.

Westwards no other major stream joins the sea until Falmouth, where the **Fal** and the smaller **Tresillian** join Carrick Roads and the busy estuary from their risings close to the A30 on the Goss Moor and near the Newlyn Downs, where the **Truro** river also begins. Another stream, the **Kenwyn**, flows through the city and the two merge with the Tresillian at the head of the estuary by Malpass. For many, many years these waters have been considered no account, but during the past 15 years a gradual change for the good has been noticed – coarse fish have appeared in the lower reaches where once they were not and I have seen some very acceptable wild brownies, and quite a lot of them, where the baby Fal runs among the china clay tips and the diggings that originally polluted it, as they did the so-called White River that runs down to the sea near St Austell. Sea trout, too, are showing in the lower river and its neighbouring Tresillian and are being fished for! With provision now in force to prevent netting in the estuaries for sea fish it is to be hoped that the migratory fish will return in numbers, also on the **Helford**, while the brown trout will certainly colonise more and more of these streams if they are allowed to. At the moment these waters remain lumped together under the name Western Rivers. These also include many tiny streams of little length that find the sea around the coasts of the heel and toe of the Peninsula. Many hold trout and fishing is by permission of the farmers. It is not until we return along the northern coast and reach Newquay that any fishing is found to attract any but the most casual of anglers. Here is the **Menalhyl**, where brown trout fishing is enjoyed by the St Mawgan Angling Club.

Two other small rivers in the area, the **Gannel** at Newquay and the **Porth** that stems from the springs that supply the reservoir of that name have sea trout runs, (sometimes many school peal can be seen in them, and some trout), as does the little river **Valency** further up the coast at Boscastle: but it is at Padstow we meet the estuary of the river **Camel**.

River Camel
For many years coupled with the Fowey as the best in the county and on occasion among the very best in the West Country, the former was said to have the edge where sea trout were concerned, while the Camel produced more salmon. In recent years figures have fluctuated and in the present climate one must take each year as it comes. However, even the most gloomy of those pessimists who foresaw doom ahead after the Lower Moor pollution near Camelford have to concede that things could be worse and give credit to the efforts being made to rehabilitate the river. All members of the river fisheries association are cooperating to back up efforts by the NRA and the three years moritorium on licensed netting in the estuary: also the recently imposed ban on netting for sea fish in the estuary – a ban that has been applied to other rivers and, hopefully, may be extended to others. The time limit for the self-imposed restrictions on rod fishing ends in 1991, as does the ban on netting by licensed netsmen but it is to be hoped that both will continue to some degree at least. Riparian owners, fishery owners and angling clubs agreed to a six weeks' delay to the start of the season to protect the smolt migration, a catch limit of two salmon in one day, four in a week and four sea trout

in a day, also setting aside certain stretches of the river as sanctuaries for the fish. Meanwhile, the NRA put fish passes in at Camelford Weir and Allenbridge to allow the fish access to the upper river and working parties from the clubs have cleared much of the rubbish accumulated in the higher river to enable salmon and sea trout to find decent spawning gravels.

The attraction of Camel for the visitor is that through membership or permit, the waters of three angling associations totalling about 15 miles of the best fishing are available, while several owners take fishing guests or are willing to lease fishing.

The river rises beyond Camelford, above Slaughter Bridge on Davidstow Moor close to the source of the Tamar tributaries Ottery and Inny, also the river Bude. Until below Camelford it is scarcely wide enough to be considered a fishing river, but has excellent gravels for spawning sea trout and salmon – a very valuable asset to future stocks so long as it is not allowed to become silted up or dammed by fallen trees and other debris or polluted by water diverted through fish farms. From Camelford various stretches on both banks are leased or owned by angling clubs, either Bodmin Anglers or Liskeard & District until the river reaches Bodmin. At the same time a twin stream, the river **Allen** follows its own valley parallel and to the west of the Camel until joining the main water near Wadebridge. The Allen is not fished very much, but is a particularly valuable nursery for sea trout. Meanwhile the Camel takes on water from several streams running down from Bodmin Moor to the east, the largest of these being the De Lank – a stream that could become a very important generator of new stock for the river if the barrier created at a quarry did not constitute such an impassable barrier for smolts, let alone the mature fish that would have to negotiate it to reach the gravels above. Like the headwaters of the Fowey, the De Lank bears little resemblance to most of the moorland streams.

It is due to the overgrown nature of most Cornish rivers that the bulk of their fish are caught by anglers plying bait or spinning lures and spoons. No holds are barred so far as legitimate baits and methods are concerned: but gradually more water is being opened up for fly fishing and this method is becoming established as the only one to be employed during the height of the sea trout season, especially during the evening and after dark. However, it will be a long time, one imagines, before worm fishing is banned altogether, although some association beats do have rules restricting anglers to artificial baits only.

After Dunmere Bridge below Bodmin town fishing on much of the Camel lies in the hands of Bodmin Anglers or the Wadebridge & District Angling Association: for the latter, water permits can be obtained from North Cornwall Angling Centre, Wadebridge, while application for membership should be made to club secretary. Membership of the Bodmin AA is limited and early application is advised to the secretary. Permits to fish club waters until the end of November can be had from the Bodmin Trading Co, D. Odgers at Dunmere and from Roger Lashbrook's Tackle, Bodmin. For the Liskeard AC waters permits can be obtained from the same outlets and those shown under River Fowey.

Bodmin Anglers have constructed a number of weirs along the middle length of water on which they own the fishing and these have proved entirely successful in holding fish during periods of low water and providing anglers with salmon they might well not otherwise catch and this improvement on the Camel's natural resources has also been carried out on an even larger scale by Tyson Jackson, a riparian owner who with his wife offers accommodation and fishing on $1^1/_2$ miles of river fairly close to the tide at Butterwell, about a mile from Nanstallon not far out of Bodmin. This is proving a most productive water and demonstrates by its results the value of such conservation, not only by offering resting places for salmon and sea trout during a hot summer – holding pools where once only a shallow, barren river ran – but encouraging a variety of wild life with otters, kingfishers, dippers and woodcock as examples. Another pleasant and often productive piece of water where fishing can be obtained by permit is higher up the river at Tresarret Manor, near Blisland.

That is the last of the river fishing available in north Cornwall until, of course, we move on to the county's share of the Upper Tamar, already considered. On the north coast of Devon there is but one major estuary and salmon fishery and that is the common outlet to the sea shared by the once renowned rivers Torridge and Taw – the land of the Two Rivers embraced by Williamson's tales of *Tarka the Otter* and *Salar the Salmon*. Apart from the almost complete dearth of salmon in the Exe for years following UDN the biggest concern for any West Country rivers has been registered as a result of the steady decline of fish stocks in both the Taw and Torridge, the latter seemingly even more sadly afflicted than the other. That the very end of the '80s began to show a faint hope for improvement was not enough to stifle the worries of many who know the rivers well: worries that were made even greater as one pollution after another (some of human making and some termed natural) set back the clock just as it seemed that the joint efforts of anglers and authority had got it going again. Netting in the joint estuary was cut by more than 50%, rod fishing was limited to the use of the fly once April was passed and a voluntary catch limit was asked of those fishing these rivers. The last few drought summers have not helped to give a clear picture, but there is still reason to believe that these once excellent rivers may gradually be restored to old glories. Tarka at least is seen to be back.

River Torridge
This is the river that changed its mind: rising only a relatively short distance to the west of the estuary at Bideford the **Torridge** heads southeast towards Dartmoor, but turns abruptly back towards the sea just before reaching Hatherleigh where it receives the tribute of the rivers **Lew** and **Okemont**. Its course runs through wild and beautiful countryside and passes the villages of Shebbear and Sheepwash. Excellent brown trout fishing is to be had here. Fishing for brownies on the upper river and for salmon and sea trout lower down can be had by permit from the Woodford Bridge Hotel at Milton Damerel (the trout fishing is by dry fly only). Another five miles of brown trouting, where wild fish are complemented by stocked trout, is available to guests at the Half Moon Inn at Sheepwash – a fishing

hotel that has been run by the Innis family since the Second World War. Fishing for salmon and sea trout is also available on lower beats. Having turned back towards Torrington the river passes close by Beaford where Gp Capt. P. Norton Smith's Little Warham fishery provides good fishing for salmon, sea trout and brownies. The lower Torridge can be very exciting when in good order and after the town of Torrington it meets the tide.

River Taw

Although twinned with Torridge in the mind the **Taw** is a different kind of river and is cradled more traditionally, high on Dartmoor close to the sources of the Okemont, East Dart, Tavy and Teign, whence it runs northwards to be joined by the **Yeo** above Eggesford and by the **Little Dart** below the village, where there is fishing for brown trout as well as migratory fish from the Fox & Hounds Hotel. This fishery extends for seven miles with easy access to all beats (each divided for two rods) from the A377. Like its neighbour, the Taw and tributaries enable fishermen to spin for salmon in March and April, after which the fly only rule is enforced, but many rods have proved this to be no handicap when conditions favour it and the fish are in.

Half way downstream from Eggesford to Umberleigh the river **Mole** joins forces and often draws a lot of running fish up to spawning beds in the **Bray** and other feeders: however, at Umberleigh all incoming salmon and sea trout enter the Rising Sun Inn beats from the sea; day permits are available to anglers when the hotel's 3$^{1}/_{2}$ miles of water are not fully booked.

At Barnstaple the Barnstaple & District AA offers limited daily permits during the week, none at weekends and bank holidays. The association has two miles of water and the contact is Mrs B. Parkin, who can also provide permits for approximately $^{3}/_{4}$ mile of brown trout fishing on both banks of Taw and Yeo above Ivy Lodge. These permits are also available from tackle shops in Barnstaple.

River Lyn

This brings us to Exmoor's precipitous and turbulent little river **Lyn** and one of the few rod fisheries managed by the National Rivers Association. It is formed by the Watersmeet Fishery leased from the National Trust and the Glenthorne Fishery. The latter can provide very good fishing for brown trout, whilst Watersmeet provides better salmon fishing. The rise and fall of this little river is rapid and its power demonstrated by the Lynmouth disaster: but the success of its fishing depends almost entirely on the fall of rain. Season, week, day and evening permits can be obtained from the Brendon House Hotel, Lynton; Lower Bourne House, Porlock; the Pet Shop, Lynton; the Kingfisher, Barnstaple. Half a mile of fishing is reserved for children, who only require a trout licence to fish a stretch between Hillsford Bridge and Watersmeet on the Hoaroak Water.

The season for salmon begins on March 1 and ends on September 30 on the Glenthorne beats and October 31 on Watersmeet. Fishing times are 8 am to sunset except during June through to September 30 when fly fishing for sea trout is permitted until 2 am between Tors Road and Rockford. Bag limits are 4 brace brown trout; 3 brace sea trout; two salmon. Fly-fishing only for trout. No worm or maggot for salmon before June and shrimp and prawn banned. No hook larger than standard 4 for bait, while weights used must not exceed $^1/_2$ oz and be lead free attached at least 18 inches from the hook.

Progressing beyond the river **Lyn** we enter the Wessex Region of the NRA and the picture changes radically. There are still plenty of trout to be found in the headwaters of the rivers running down from the hills to the flat wetlands of Somerset and Avon, where their kind are replaced by the excellent coarse fish that provide so much sport in the slower, deeper rivers. There is good trout fishing in the foothills of Exmoor, the Quantocks, Mendips and Cotswolds: but this is at a premium and we consider this matter again when dealing with the coarse fishing opportunities in the region and those clubs with some trout waters available to members.

As far as fishing for salmon and sea trout is concerned this is entirely restricted to the chalk rivers of the Avon & Dorset area and these, again, are referred to in the chapter on coarse fishing.

The Cotswolds

Much of the trout fishing offered by the Cotswolds' streams is reserved by the landowners or for the restricted membership of a few clubs, chief of which is Cotswold Fly Fishers who have some seven miles of double and single bank on the river **Windrush** from Burford to Minster Lovell and at Stanton Harcourt, also on the rivers Coln and Leach. Membership is restricted to 155 rods for which there is a waiting list and, I have on authority, a probable waiting time of some six years! However, if I were younger and lived a wee bit closer to that area where I was happily able to fish many miles of those delectable rivers when I lived among the wolds, I would certainly make a point of being on that list.

At Worsham one mile of single bank is held by Witney Angling Society's trout section, but again membership is limited to 40 and there is a waiting list. Both clubs stock their waters with brown trout and rainbows and limit fishing to the use of fly, dry and wet.

However, on the river **Coln** there is opportunity to fish some 500 yards of this, in my view, even more delightful stream for residents at the Swan Hotel at Bibury and the charge is purely nominal to cover the cost of the NRA licence: and a little downstream at the Bibury Court Hotel 700 yards of fishing is available to residents only. Both stretches hold stocked browns and rainbows and the use of dry fly and nymph only permitted.

At Fairford the Bull Hotel still offers the trout fishing for which it has been renowned for decades back to the time when the present stillwater opportunities only existed at Blagdon Lake. Today there are $1^1/_2$ miles double bank where a day permit can be had for about £15 and a half day for half price. Of course, the hotel's guests enjoy a reduction. Again these waters are stocked annually with both brownies and rainbows. Closer to its meeting with the Thames the Coln at

GAME FISHING RIVERS

Whelford to Dudsgrove offers members of the Cotswold Fly Fishers a mile of double and single bank.

The third river is the **Leach** which emerges as a trickle from the hills by Northleach on the A40 and joins the Thames at Lechlade and Cotswold Fly Fishers have a mile of double bank fly fishing for wild brownies at Little Faringdon, while the Lechlade Trout Fishery has a short stretch of the river as well as its major trout fly fishing operations on an 11 acre lake.

Sources for River Fishing Permits

Do not forget to enclose a stamped addressed envelope when seeking information and applying for permits, when you should also enclose the requisite cost.

Avon
Avon FA
19 Stella Road, Preston, Paignton

D. M. Blake
Fore Street, Totnes

O'Neil
55 Church Street, Kingsbridge

Post Office
Loddiswell, Nr Kingsbridge

Axe
Cownhayne Farm
Colyton
Tel: Colyton 52267

Camel
Bodmin AA
Ray Burrows, 26 Meadow Place, Bodmin
Tel: Bodmin 5513

Bodmin Trading Co
Church Square, Bodmin

Coomb Mill Leisure Ltd
K. Field, St Breward
Tel: Bodmin 850344

Tyson Jackson
Butterwell, Nanstallon
Tel: Lanivet 831515

Liskeard & District AC
O. G. Gilbert, 11 Richmond Road, Pelynt, Nr Looe
or
T. Sobey (Treasurer)
Trevartha, Liskeard

North Cornwall Angling Centre
1 Egloshayle Road, Wadebridge

D. Odgers
Gwendreath, Dunmere, Bodmin

W. W. Pope
Tressaret Manor, Nr Blisland.
Tel: Bodmin 850338

Roger Lashbrook's Tackle
West End Garage, Bodmin

Wadebridge & District AA
A. T. Gill
Jasmine Cottage, St Mabyn
Tel: St Mabyn 508

Dart
Arundell Arms Hotel
Lifton
Tel: Lifton 84666/84244

Badgers Holt Restaurant
Dartmeet

Charles Bingham
West Down, Whitchurch, Nr Tavistock

James Bowden & Son
Chagford

Church House Inn
Holne

Drum Sports
Newton Abbot
Tel: Newton Abbot 65333

Erme Flies
Ermington, Nr Ivybridge

The Forest Inn
Hexworthy

Mabins News
Buckfastleigh

Plainmoor Angling Centre
Torquay

Princehall Hotel
Two Bridges

Sea Trout Inn
Staverton

38 A CONCISE GUIDE TO WEST COUNTRY FISHING

The Shop
Poundsgate

Two Bridges Hotel
Princetown

Wheeler's Sports Shop
Totnes

Erme
Mill Leat Trout Farm
Ermington, Ivybridge
Tel: Modbury 830560

Exe
The Bakery
Hemyock

Carnarvon Arms Hotel
Dulverton
Tel: Dulverton 23302

Crediton FFC
Tel: Crediton 3270

Exeter Angling Centre
Smythen Street, Exeter
Tel: Exeter 36404

Exmoor Forest Hotel
Simonsbath
Tel: Exford 341

Fisherman's Cot
Bickleigh Bridge, Tiverton
Tel: Bickleigh 237/289

M. J. Ford
Country Sports, Tiverton
Tel: Tiverton 254770

Lance Nicholson Tackle
Dulverton
Tel: Dulverton 23409

John Sharpe
Parlour Cottage, Exbridge
Tel: Dulverton 23104

Tarr Steps Hotel
Hawkridge
Tel: Winsford 293

Upper Culm FA
'Sunset', Clayhidon,
Exeter

Fowey
Angling Centre
6 Victoria Place, St Austell

M. I. Barker
Rivermead Farm,
Twowatersfoot
Tel: Cardinham 464

Bodmin Trading
Company
see under Camel

Cormorant Hotel
Golant

Doney & Hancock
Fore Street, Callington

Forways Autos
The Quay, Lostwithiel

Fowey Marine
North Street, Fowey

Godfrey's Stores
Barn Street, Liskeard

Ken Raymond (Tackle)
Lower Lux Street,
Liskeard

Lanhydrock AA
Lanhydrock Park, Bodmin
Tel: Bodmin 4281

Liskeard & District AC
see under Camel

Lostwithiel FA
J. H. Hooper, 4 Reeds
Park, Lostwithiel

Mike Summers Angling
Centre
Newport, Launceston

Post Office
Rilla Mill, Calington

Post Office
Tideford, Saltash

Sam's Fishing & Camping
Supplies
East Looe

Tropical & Pet Supplies
East Looe

Lyn
Brendon House Hotel
Lynton

The Kingfisher
22 Castle Street,
Barnstaple

Lower Bourne House
Porlock

Pet Shop
Lee Road, Lynton

Watersmeet & Glenthorne
Fisheries
managed by NRA

Lyner, Looe & Seaton
see under Fowey

Menalhyl
St Mawgan AC
T. J. Trevenna, Lanvean
House, St. Mawgan,
Newquay

Otter
Deer Park Hotel
Weston, Honiton
Tel: Honiton 41266/7

Otter Inn
Honiton
Tel: Honiton 2594

Plym
DK Sports
The Barbican, Plymouth

Plymouth & District
Freshwater AA
D. L. Owen
Tel: Plymouth 705033

Rock Stores
Yelverton

Tavy, Walkham & Plym
FC
Ian Parker
Tel: Plymouth 263010

Tacklists in Plymouth

Tamar
Arundell Arms Hotel
see under Dart

Ray Beare Sports
Bude

Bude AA
29 West Park Road, Bude

DIY Centre
The Square, Holsworthy

Endsleigh House Hotel
Milton Abbot
Tel: Milton Abbot 248

Mike Summers Angling
Centre
see under Fowey

Tavy
see under Plym

GAME FISHING RIVERS

Taw
Barnstaple & District AA
A. J. Penny
Endswell House
Raleigh Road
Barnstaple

Tackle shops in Barnstaple

Fox & Hounds Hotel
Eggesford
Tel: Chumleigh 80345

Rising Sun Inn
Umberleigh
Tel: High Bickington 60447
Note: this property, inn and fishery was for sale as separate items at the time of writing

Teign
Bowden's in the Square
Chagford

Clifford Bridge Caravan Park

Drum Sports
see under Dart

Exeter Angling Centre
see under Exe

Lower Teign FA
Lower Brook Street,
Teignmouth
Tel: Teignmouth 2133/4
or

P. M. Knibbs
Morningside
Long Lane
Shaldon
Tel. (after 6 pm): Shaldon 873612

Mill End Hotel
Sandypark

Percy Lodge
Newton Abbot

Steps Bridge Hotel
Tel: Christow 52310

Upper Teign FA
The Anglers Rest, Fingle Bridge, Drewsteignton

J. Getliff
22 The Square
Chagford
Tel: Chagford 433493

Torridge
Half Moon Inn
Sheepwash, Beaworthy
Tel: Black Torrington 376

Little Warham Water
Beaford, Winkleigh
Tel: Winkleigh 317

Woodford Bridge
Milton Damerel, Holsworthy
Tel: Milton Damerel 481

The Cotswolds

Coln
Bibury Court Hotel
Bibury, Nr Cirencester
Tel: Bibury 337

Bull Hotel
Fairford
Tel: Cirencester 71 2535

Cotswold FFC
F. Cord, Membership Secretary
7 St Lawrence Road, South Hinksey
Tel: Oxford 086573

Swan Hotel
Bibury, Nr Cirencester
Tel: Bibury 204

Leach
Cotswold FFC
as above

Windrush
Cotswold FFC
as above

Witney Angling Society
Michael Mann
86 Early Road, Witney
Tel: Witney 702587

# 4

FISHING FOR STILLWATER TROUT

This branch of the sport is fairly simply divided into fisheries stocked regularly with takeable trout, whether brownies, rainbows or both, and those waters where brown trout and in some cases rainbows are introduced at a smaller stage and left to grow on to become sporting quarry. In the first the fisherman who buys his permit will know that all being well the fish are there to enable him to catch whatever limit the fishery allows – a limit that varies from one big rainbow on some private waters to eight at established lakes like Chew Valley and Blagdon and six on the Wessex and South West Water companies' stocked reservoirs.

The fish of the stocked reservoirs are bred at hatcheries and reared to around the pound mark (with a smattering of much larger ones) and have been fed on high protein pellets until their release into what is their new and often very temporary home, where they begin to adjust themselves to the available stocks of natural food. Obviously, where rod pressure is heavy and conditions enable the patrons to take many of these rainbows out almost as soon as they are put in, some fish may well be caught before they have time to investigate the natural larder and the capture of these mature but inexperienced rainbow stockies is made the easier for equally inexperienced anglers by their willingness to have a go at the most unlikely offerings ... in many cases lures that resemble nothing but the concoction of feathers, tinsel and assorted materials that they are.

The rainbow's downfall is further assisted by the obvious nature of the fish which will take into its mouth items that bear no resemblance whatever to the natural prey around them: aggravation or aggression, but whatever the motive force it certainly speeds the rainbow's end!

For some years now a method of fishing has become known as Cornish Knitting. For this purpose the angler casts out his lure or lures as far as possible, tucks the rod under his arm and uses both hands to strip the line back to him just as fast as he can, bringing the lures back at a speed faster than any real foodstuffs move below the surface and almost too fast for the fish to catch them! It is a most artificial kind of fishing despite an often wild setting: but I have been a little over-critical. It is after all the fishing that makes the fisherman and if the new rod is content to remain an immature fisherman after he has caught his first trout, then he will have little complaint if the rainbows remain small and unworldly ... just as long as they keep coming to his lures!

But not all the stockies give themselves up: some are hunted down and killed by heron, cormorant, mink and otter; but some survive to remain unscathed through the winter and if the elements are kind will greet the spring of a new season as worthy quarry – a very different kettle of fish, the over-wintered rainbow!

Some fisheries acclimatise the stock, moving them into holding ponds where the food ration of pellets is reduced as natural insects become available and trout of this kind, too, are a worthier quarry when eventually transferred to the fishing area. The jumbo rainbows that provide a lake with its reputation for big fish are usually put in as they are taken out – big fish. If they are not caught by an angler fairly quickly they may well remain elusive for weeks and, if the food supply is good, will become like their over-wintered brothers and a prize worth winning when caught towards the back-end of the year.

I tend to look on our sport as seasonal and feel that somehow it loses some of its appeal when carried on through the best part of a year, even all year. It is better to say 'through the most of a year' because the best part of it is in the months of May and June, then again in September, where rainbows are concerned. July and August have their moments, but all too often the main hatches of fly occur towards the end of the day and the hours for fishing are curtailed. This is the time, too, when high water temperatures and bright sunlight drive fish out of the shallower areas near the banks of most reservoirs and into the cooler depths, making a boat and probably a sinking line necessities if the rod is to follow his quarry.

The art of fishing these well-stocked stillwaters is to seek the larger trout and catch them on the representation of the natural insects or fry they may be feeding on ... and catch them consistently. This takes a dedicated angler – a person of eagle eye and observation and the power to cast his flies as thistledown: someone who has studied and understands the ways of fish and of the creatures on which they feed! We are not short of such artists in the West Country.

But for a while let us consider the problems facing the angler who fishes the 'natural' waters and so-called Budget Fisheries, where the main quarry may well be those brownies first entered as fingerlings and now grown on to anything from ³/₄ lb to 3 lb with some being caught in the 5 lb mark, while there is evidence in every form but the fish itself of Leviathan prowling in the depths beyond range of the bank.

Some of these fisheries are zoned for fishing with fly, spinner and bait: others are strictly limited to the use of the fly and it is this method which I now consider in the light of considerable discussion with some of the most successful fishermen, whose record on such waters has been too markedly consistent to be ignored. Prior to the 1990 West of England Open Championships – held on a wild water for the first time in eleven years – I talked with those who had fished this venue at Colliford Lake on Bodmin Moor since it first opened in 1986 in order to provide some sort of guide to competitors with little knowledge of the problems confronting them and, since this advice is mainly applicable to all fisheries of this kind, it seems well worth-while offering it to a wider audience now.

To attain success in the field of 'wild' country sports of any kind it is necessary to understand the habits of the quarry – be it beast, fish or fowl – and the first difference between the tame rainbow trout and the wild brownie is that the latter is much more territorial than its Californian cousin. In rivers the brown trout has a secure home or holt under the bank or some overhanging rock or bed of weeds from which it moves into more open water at feeding time and back to which it bolts when hooked! The browns of stillwaters also have their retreats and patrol for food over a fairly restricted area. And anyone who has contacted a big brown trout will have experienced that almost unstoppable rush of the fish back to its lair when hooked – a powered drive towards safety that very often leads to breakage and another tale to carry home!

The rainbow stockies, however, are more inclined to stay in shoals of similar size and to cruise over so wide an area that anglers are content to stand as steady as herons and wait for the trout to come to them!

In fact, at the championships referred to I watched no less than twenty rods share an area of bank no more than 300 yards in length and hold position for most of the day, casting repeatedly over the limited area in front of them. It is absolutely true that the onlooker sees most of the game and at the end of the day, when results were analysed, it did not surprise me to find that of 92 competitors a bare 34 had caught the 67 trout taken during seven hours of fishing.

It was also no surprise to find that those who caught fish were those who hunted them and found them at home instead of waiting rather hopelessly for a willing brown trout to come to them, having already scared the local fish off by their repeated casting!

Colliford Lake offers the angler some twelve miles of bank to explore and it is a fifty minute walk to the furthest part which for obvious reasons remain the least exploited. However, the fishery has no real 'hot spots' and a fish may be seen moving close to the bank just below the one permit hut and half an hour's quiet hunt along a bank in any direction may carry you past several hundred trout, some of which may well be on the feed, even if they are not showing at the surface. And your permit only allows you to take four . . .

But choose a spot on the bank, even worse wade deep into the lake and stay there for an hour and after the first fishless ten minutes you may just as well not bother to tire your arms with any more casting – your potential quarry will have retired to less disturbed areas of deeper water beyond casting range and not many other fish are likely to come cruising by.

So, whilst I like to wear thigh waders to enable me to kneel in damp grass or shallow margins to cast along the edge of the water to fish shrimping close to the bank, wade only when it is necessary to cross a small runlet or avoid an obstacle in your path along the bank.

Yes, the consultants were single-minded on these two points: do NOT wade and do NOT become rooted to one spot! And again they are totally agreed on the need for a versatile and stealthy approach where banks are bereft of cover as they are on many moorland waters, whilst other smaller fisheries, well-bushed, equally demand subtle fieldcraft. Any angler suddenly looming against the horizon round natural cover will not go unnoticed by the trout!

The ability to cast a long line is not so important as the versatility needed to give your line a cross-country route, over rough grass, heather and ling to enable the fly to reach a shrimp-feeding brownie moving in shallow water: you may have to make that cast from a matter of ten yards up the bank to a fish stationed only feet from the edge of the water!

Anything other than a cautious approach along the bank, observing the surface of the lake ahead close to the bank for the least tell-tale of trout activity will lead to opportunities being lost when you see the wave of a big trout break away from the shallows.

For the young and eagle-eyed the signs of feeding trout may be clearly defined once they are understood: sometimes a fin or tail will break the surface, on occasion trout will head-and-tail or porpoise-roll and on others there will be a great swirl or a slashing rise that splashes gleaming droplets of water into the air; but the only sign of a sipping take can be a tiny dimple on the surface or a small bubble of air. Sometimes a fish feeding sub-surface may only register this activity by the most slight and subtle humping of the water, even some slight change in the surface pattern that is seen, but cannot really be described! The thing is that you will know it when you see it, but acute eyesight does not serve all of us forever and rather than lose this great advantage over the fish and ability that enhances the pleasure of the sport to such a great degree I do advise investment in a pair of those excellent lightweight binoculars now available to us. Such a pair will amplify those other joys of your surroundings that are not in themselves fishing, but essentially an integral part of the pleasure of the sport.

One of my models for this thesis is that excellent angler Paul Netherton, whose ability at contests to be the first to return to the scales with a limit catch is indisputable. He stresses our points so far, saying, 'The best fish will feed within a few feet of the bank, even in bright sunshine.' But another top angler, Paul Meredith (the Television South West angling presenter) advises, 'The brown is basically a cold water fish and will tend to frequent the deeper cooler areas during the day, coming into the shallower bank areas in morning and evening to feed.'

With the exception of the general principles already dealt with the approach by each man is completely opposite: while that of a third top model – as it were – is at variance with both, although probably following Paul Netherton's line more nearly than that of Paul Meredith. He is Eddy Chambers who was West of England Champion in 1987 and 1989 but unable to defend his title in 1990 because of injuries sustained in a motor accident a week before the event. In one way Eddy agrees with the suggestion that during the hours of full daylight trout in the shallows should be ignored because the angler is more likely to spook them than catch them. The early hours and late evening are a different proposition and he changes his approach to suit the occasion. Like Paul Netherton he is a man who uses small flies, mainly sizes 14 or 16, although sometimes turning to size 12 when emulating the larger naturals, sometimes going down to size 18 when some especially small insect appears on or in the water and becomes the main ingredient of the trout diet. Paul Meredith, who enjoys great success in the somewhat different conditions of Stithians Reservoir near Redruth, is more of a lure man, saying that in extreme cases lures of four inches in length are not too big, but conceding that at certain times of the year smaller offerings will prove successful. For example he suggests that by September a long-haired lure like a Collie Dog tied to a size 6 single hook and about three inches long will be enough.

What of fish following such a lure and tweaking the tail? Paul says that most brownies will take this offering solidly at the head end, not attacking the tail as do small perch or peal or small brown trout for that matter. In fact it is quite nerve-wracking to watch the wave of a big brown trout following the path of the lure towards shallow water ... what do you do? Do you slow the pace of the retrieve, do you speed it up or do you carry on at the same level pace?

There is absolutely no answer to this question: all options have succeeded and all have failed at some time or another and the ball is very much in the angler's court. How he plays it is solely up to him and sometimes he is lucky. Where lures are concerned the way you fish them is more important than the actual fly and as a rule the colour you like is the one that will probably catch fish: but where the water is peaty or coloured, certain colours show up better than others and yellow, hot orange and the extremes of black and white usually work better than others. Meredith stresses the need for these to be long and slim and suggests Maribou as the best material to dress them because of its lifelike shimmer. Also he believes that the addition of some fluorescent material can help you to score on occasion.

Apart from these comparatively huge attractors there is a medium range to be considered from those well-tried traditionals of the past – Mallard & Claret, Peter Ross, Greenwell's Glory and Wickham's Fancy among them – to now well-established favourites and proven killers like the Montana Nymph, Soldier Palmer, Viva and Black & Peacock Spider. I have not mentioned the Invicta in its various guises or the famed but not infallible Alexandra: they are traditional, but the first seems to be extremely successful when Sedges are hatching and the second kills trout when they are fry-feeding, also when feeding on the Coryxa or Water Boatman.

In the range of wet flies, too, are such patterns as Pheasant Tail Nymph and Gold Ribbed Hare's Ear (abbreviated to PTN and GRHE), which with others do suggest to the fish some of the natural insects upon which they feed – especially the olive tribe.

Here we move to the end of the spectrum extreme from the lures – the dry fly and those that are fished in or just beneath the surface film and suggest the insects available to the fish at the time. The naturals will vary with the different kinds and qualities of water – some hate acidity while others thrive in pH of 4, 5, and 6. There are other creatures common to all stillwaters and different seasons, mainly those terrestrials blown from the land like hawthorn and heather flies and black gnats, an assortment of beetles varying from a pinhead size to an inch in length and coloured from shining black to fluorescent green or a vivid red. There are migrating ants on the wing and lumbering daddy-longlegs, grasshoppers as well as the frogs and newts that come to spawn in early spring and fall prey to marauding brownies: a friend of mine caught a $2^1/_2$ lb fish with three frogs in its stomach, each a full eight inches in length. And, of course, the time of the tadpoles arrives and a little later the hatching of coarse fish fry.

But in general the insects that create the most surface activity among hungry trout on a majority of stillwaters are the chironomids. These are diptera, closely akin to the mosquitoes and gnats, who follow a cycle from egg through a larval stage known as the bloodworm, then the midge pupa, from which at the surface emerges the insect leaving its empty case or shuck behind in uncountable masses which often drift with the wind and pile up against the shore in what can only be described as millions. At all its stages is the developing insect a food for fish, copied by the fisherman and used at various depths and in different ways to imitate the natural behaviour of the creature. It is the ultimate stage that proves most difficult when the hordes of perfect midges – known as Buzzers at that stage because of the noise the swarms make when concentrating around one's head – return to the water to deposit their eggs and die on the surface. This often occurs when it is too dark to see clearly enough any actual rise to your own artificial lying among dozens of naturals, which also makes the chance of the trout selecting the artificial the less!

Actually anglers seem to use the word Buzzer as a general term to refer to the midge pupa and it is this distinctive shape that is mostly used – the slim segmented body, wing cases and breathing tubes copied everywhere in all colours and by many means, some extremely ingenious, some simple beyond belief: but not quite as simple as a naked hook painted red or with a thin piece of rubber band whipped on the shank to emulate the bloodworm!

Chironomids are among the first insects to populate a new sheet of water, not quite as quickly as the coryxa, perhaps, but their breeding rate is such as to establish a valuable supply of fish foods in a remarkably short time and to draw the trout towards the surface where most fly fishermen want them to be. In their different sizes and colours this variety alone provides the angler with a problem of discovering just which kind is on the water *and* attracting fish.

The time of any one variety may be no longer than that of the mayfly or seasonal terrestrials like hawthorn and daddy-longlegs, but as one ends so another starts, sometimes overlapping, and, all lumped together, the chironomids in their varying forms provide a more than useful fisherman's fly for most of the brown trout season.

Anglers fishing a Buzzer rise usually use a leader with three flies and the general consensus is for a long rod, a light line, a leader between 13 and 15 ft in length. Where once the tapered cast was preferred by many who believed it enabled them to produce a gentler cast using a single fly, the use of three flies allows a level leader to reach out and turn over nicely: while the same applies to lure fishermen using a heavy artificial on a level leader up to 25 ft long. Lure fishermen also tend to employ heavier lines than those preferred when fishing the dry fly or using nymphs, wet patterns, midge and sedge pupae and of course where winter fishing is permitted or the trout have retreated to the depths to seek a greater comfort than the overheated or icy shallows provide it may be necessary to 'trawl the bottom' with heavy lures at the end of a sinking – even weighted – line.

For that time through from spring to autumn when natural fly life close to and on the surface calls for the use of the smaller patterns, a rod of 11 to $11^1/_2$ ft is preferred so long as it will easily cast a line of AFTM rating 5 or 6. To this is attached a leader not much longer than the rod, level and of a breaking strain between 3 and 6 lb. The strength of the end tackle must depend to some extent on the size of the trout likely to be encountered and the degree to which the fishery is full or free of hazards ... a man five foot tall (even a child) can tame a powerful swimmer at the end of a light rod just so long as there is plenty of clear water to play him in!

Once securely hooked the immediate danger a good trout poses is in its rush to reach that cover it has grown to look on as a safe refuge. If the fisherman can hold that powered dive for weedbed, roots, rocks or other hidden snags (and any further rushes that may materialise) the only other problems will come when the trout starts fighting on the surface or the hook-hold wears during a prolonged struggle. With both trout and salmon, having survived the first immediate problems in the early stage of the battle, I tend to put severe pressure on the fish for a short while just to ascertain that the hook is securely home after which I play my prize as firmly as I may without bringing him to the surface – where I want him only when he is beaten and on his side ready to be drawn to the landing net or beached!

For many years now angling writers have followed the rule of fishing fine and far off ... that advice is as good today as ever it was and its first element is far simpler today than it was. Modern monofilament nylon has lent a strength to the finest thread undreamed of in the days when gut formed the cast and was graded first by size or diameter, then on the X scale. For instance, measured as 1/1000 ths of inch, .007 was the equivalent of 4X and expected to stand a strain of 2 lb; 3X or .009 would handle 3 lb. Today, however, we speak in terms of breaking strains only, the diameter of the nylon varying just as the old gut did from one manufacturer's product to another. But today, as I said, nylon does give the angler a greater advantage: for instance, Maxima (which I tend to use because it has a certain rigidity) of the equivalent diameter to the old 4X gut has a breaking strain of 4 lb and is almost invisible in water. Apart from its obvious link with James Bond, modern .007 is licensed to kill!

I chose that particular breaking strain because it is the one recommended by the experts for our purpose, added to which a new version known as double strength nylon will give you the same breaking strain for half the diameter. Eddy Chambers recommends this but concedes that some people cannot get on with it and suggests the use of 3 lb BS Drennan in its place.

Before applying the outfit let us for a moment consider one set of equipment used by one of the most successful stillwaters fly fishermen. His rod is an 11 ft 7 in carbon fibre carrying a $3^1/_2$ in reel, No 6 double-tapered floating line and a 13 ft leader to which the top dropper is attached five feet from the nylon's union with the line: the second dropper is tied a further four feet down and the tail fly is tied to the leader's end – obviously another four feet on! When I saw Paul Netherton he had landed two brace (the limit) of brown trout between $1^1/_4$ and $1^3/_4$ lb in 25 minutes' patrol along Colliford's east bank, starting at 8.50 pm. It was mid-August and the lake became alive with rising fish. The flies that did the damage then were a Rough Olive (12) as top dropper or Bob Fly, an Olive Buzzer (14) on the next dropper and a Red Buzzer (14) at the tail. The in-colour for dry flies at the time was hot orange or red, but this can vary with the season and the in-colour can be black, brown, claret, green or yellow.

Eddy Chambers' tackle varies slightly. His rod at 11 ft 3 in is shorter, his size 5 line is slightly lighter and is weight-forward and his preference for the dry fly is even greater than Paul's: but both men agree that while the maxim of fishing fine applies the need to fish far off does not ... well not much of the time. Why cast to distant fish when there are equally takeable trout closer to you? One advantage of long casting when fishing from a bank bereft of any cover is the fact that your shape does not come within the trout's cone of vision, while the fish close to shore will undoubtedly see and hear you unless you approach it with the greatest care!

Eddy, as we saw earlier, is not in favour of fishing close to the bank during the day because the danger of spooking the quarry becomes greater as the day becomes brighter: but the picture changes as the light fades, in the early morning and when underwater vision is blurred by a good wave riding the surface above it.

There is one point about tackle where my model differs from others – the dropper connection. For countless years the pundits have advised the use of droppers of some four or five inches in length: he prefers to use connections to the leader almost twice that length for the reason that this gives each fly an identity of its own and lessens the chance of trout hitting the leader when aiming for the Bob or middle fly.

It is for this reason that Paul Meredith chooses to fish with one fly. He told me, 'So many times I hear people say that they have had a lot of pulls, but that the fish are not taking properly: invariably they are using droppers and the trout are not hitting the fly but the line.' Wild fish can be very fast takers and often not very good shots!

It is to this fast, savage rise that the other Paul refers when he advises the angler NOT to strike, but tighten, as, of course, we always should. Anything in the way of a hard reaction to the already heavy take will lead to broken nylon and a lost fish. In any case there is no need for a swift reaction to a rising stillwaters trout.

Stillwater Rainbows

In October 1990 a rainbow trout weighting $8^{1}/_{2}$ lb as near as dammit was caught by Harold Pearson from Siblyback Lake near Liskeard: it was at the time the best rainbow taken from a South West Water plc reservoir during the season and took a black tandem lure presented by the retired printer, secretary of his local club and treasurer of the Devon & Cornwall Federation. This lure, maybe an imitation of the black leech on which trout will feed at the bottom, was tied on two size 10 hooks and attached to a 4 lb breaking strain leader: but when the contents of the trout's stomach were examined there was no evidence at all of recent feeding, no clue to what the fish had been taking.

I refer to this incident because it does bear out the fact that towards the back-end of the year the larger trout, both browns and rainbows, do turn to feeding on shoals of minnows, sticklebacks and coarse fish fry that throng some waters and the use of the lure may well be the only way of trying to catch them.

After successive drought summers and mild winters the fry appear in shoals much earlier than usual, pinheads at first but growing rapidly until they are in fact small fish three or four inches long. In such seasons the bigger fish turn their attention to this diet earlier than usual and by the time of the Fall they may well be feeding exclusively on roach or perch that need the large lure recommended by Meredith to represent the prey.

Most anglers associate the great shoals of fry with shallows around the bank or the edges of islands – the places where earlier the tadpoles will have swarmed. When trout move into these shallows the violence of their raids is clearly to be seen: however, at lakes like Chew and Blagdon and others, of course, 'wolf packs' of large trout sometimes gather to carry out combined attacks on shoals of bigger juveniles that have moved into deeper water and this phenomena was clearly to be seen at the Midland's big Rutland Water this year, when flocks of gulls circled and swooped over the scene of such slaughter of the innocents – as we more commonly associate them to do when mackerel and bass are hunting the britt at sea! Obviously a big lure is demanded for such big occasions...

This scenario is one extreme of a wide range of techniques employed by fly fishermen during the year, the other being that period when the tiniest of artificials are presented to the trout in the gentlest possible way with the most careful approach – the high time of the dry fly or those insects hatching or waiting to hatch just below or within the surface film.

However, small fish or no small fish for prey, there are other times when the trout must be sought in deep water, when the temperature of their surroundings dictates this and when the natural animal life upon which they feed is limited severely to those creepy-crawly creatures that exist on or close to the bed of the lake – the leech, for instance, the caddis grubs or larvae of the sedge flies, water snails and shrimps. This is during the winter months and those of early spring when the seasonal fisheries see the start to a new season – a time when if a humble beginner wants to catch his limit he is most likely to achieve that ambition and catch averages from almost all reservoirs hit a high they are rarely likely to repeat that year! It is the time of the lure and, probably, the sinking line.

It is also a time when it is manifestly demonstrated that, despite their ignorance, the most recently introduced stocky rainbow is able to tolerate concentrated heavy casting by a line of fishers crowding the bank space almost shoulder to shoulder for just so long ... not indefinitely. Sport, often fast and furious to begin with, has shown a marked tendency to decrease as the day goes on and to cease altogether by midday. The inexperienced rainbows have now gained an experience for which they have little liking and gradually moved out of the range of the thrashing lines! At least, that is how I have seen it to be in the West Country over more than fifteen years.

Despite that, the spring start does offer the tyro a very good chance to draw first blood and, besides the host of newly introduced small fish in the 1 lb range, just a chance of contacting one of those bigger fish that have over-wintered in the reservoir. Except after a severe winter these are superb trout, fully restored to that fully-tailed, bright silver condition we so admire. Conditions usually make this a time for lures, but these need not be of the magnitude demanded five months later when the trout have turned to fish feeding! As a last comment on this subject so far as a concentration of fishermen is concerned, I have noted over the years that angling commentators usually find a reason for a decline in sport as the opening day progresses and this may vary from a change in direction or intensity of the wind, absence of cloud, a sudden rise or fall in temperature and so on, but rarely the correct one. That is, too much casting by too many Rods in too restricted an area.

During the next ten to fifteen years new lures will be added to the already overcrowded list that has grown during the past decade or so: but among the latter the Viva must be mentioned. Simply a black body and hackle with a green tag, this lure has achieved prominence steadily since it first began to prove its value in the late 'seventies: but I think it is probable that the appearance of the Montana nymph in the mid-eighties has had an even greater impact. The use of either or both is more than likely to provide success and their use in sizes 6 to 14 fairly close to the surface as the water warms on a fine April day, or at the end of a lead-core line in thirty feet of water when the conditions are bitter, or later when the shallows have heated to an unbearable degree and trout have withdrawn to the cooler deeps, provide their exponents with equal success.

Obviously there are many other lures for these occasions, but in those early days I have found the accent for success heavily pitched on 'something black'.

It is, I think, worth mentioning the fact that – regardless of what method or type of fly is used – boat anglers tend to enjoy their sport more consistently through the day and that those coming late on the scene seem to find the trout slightly restored from their shock, more composed and prepared to cooperate again: but a March or April day ends early anyway and the trout may well go off the feed long before dusk, British Summer Time or not.

Another brief comment for this part of the year. Quite often the floating line and the dry fly will prove effective for a brief period during the day – sometimes providing surprising and spectacular results: but it should be remembered that various members of the great olive family can hatch out on any day of the year, especially when the upper layers of water have been warmed by the sun. Gone are the days when your line either sank or floated and sometimes just one line was made to do both as required. With all forms of fishing tackle the line has undergone the same revolution that was brought about by the explosion of both stillwaters and their fishermen during the past thirty years. Can there be any doubt that it was this and the interest generated that made experiment and invention well worth the developers while?

The beautiful silk lines of the long-ago have been replaced by a wide range of plastic coated substitutes, each designed to fill a particular purpose. Of course, we still have the floaters, but they vary not only in weights and sizes but in purpose, which may be accuracy, delicacy or distance. Then there are those floating lines to which a varying length of sinking line may be attached, while the sinkers themselves go through a range of densities from the intermediate with its slow descent through the water to the heavy lead-core line that more or less plummets to the bottom.

The intermediate line is of neutral density and is the ideal equipment for those fishing with artificial midge or sedge pupae, nymphs and small wet flies, especially if they do not enjoy employing a very long monofilament leader on a floater. The rate of descent of the intermediate is about six inches in five seconds as against an average rate of one to two feet a second for the fast sinking line. These very heavy lines can be difficult to control and are only suitable for fishing very deep water from a boat or the bank on those few fisheries where the latter shelves sharply, as may be the case on some flooded quarries etc. In any case, the line you use must be balanced to your rod and modern rods are marked with the weight of line they are designed to take.

Before we leave the realm of lures it should be noted that the use of these is not suitable in small fisheries, not in the larger sizes at least and many waters have a restriction on the size of hooks used – usually size 10 long shank.

As water warms and the light hours grow longer, their message is received by many creatures hitherto hidden in the mud or gravel or the weeds, and activity increases among those insects now at that stage prior to hatching as imago at the surface and of these the earliest and most numerous may well be the chironomids, which we talked about earlier.

For a period the angler may still have to fish the deeper water, but mostly not deeper than twelve feet and it is worth knowing just how quickly your lure, nymph or pupa imitation sinks. A simple matter of counting is usually sufficient to tell you when to begin to retrieve the artificial as was one day illustrated at Upper Tamar Lake by John Mitchell, author of *Stillwater Trout*. He took a brace of lovely rainbows, each about 6 lb, 'on a count of 25' as he recalls. As the season moves on so the insects and the fish move nearer the surface, you have less water to search before finding the 'taking' depth and fishing becomes much easier using an intermediate or floating line: even when no fish may be showing at the surface.

There is a mistaken belief that if the trout are not in evidence then they are not feeding: if the insects are not hatching then they are not active; but as anyone who has fished clear trout streams or the crystal waters of spring fed lakes (where weed beds, usually abundant and rich in their verdant health harbour a mass of insect-life) will know, trout can be active well down in the water while the food stock is there. I have noticed over the past few years that more often than not fish caught from such a fishery, Rockbourne near Fordingbridge, are taken within the first three feet from the surface. This also applies to lakes whose character makes it impossible to observe the movements of our quarry.

The various stages from larva to perfect insect can be represented by artificial flies – the fierce looking larvae of the dragonfly, then its nymphs and those of the damselfly: the stick fly stage of the sedge and its pupa, rising through the water to hatch into the adult fly that often scutters across the surface before take-off: the delicate bloodworms that become the pupa of the chironomid and are imitated by a bare hook painted red or yellow, a length from a rubber band whipped on to the hook shank, to be replaced by the insect's penultimate stage, wrongly known as 'buzzers', then the emerging insect and finally that stage which provided the insect with the name as swarms 'buzz' about inland bushes and around the angler's head before returning to the water to lay their eggs and start the cycle all over again.

For a number of natural reasons certain waters are preferred to others by some insects and crustaceans: some may hold an abundance of shrimp and snails, while others have few of these but host a whole mass of chironomids; others can earn a great reputation for the numbers of dragonflies and damsels to be seen there and the artificial of the nymphs succeed more consistently than elsewhere, while the same can be said of the sedges abounding at other lakes. The very brief appearance of the mayfly is limited to waters in the east of the region, but there is some evidence that these large flies are extending their range into the west, even as far as some of Cornwall's rivers.

Of course, some of the problems confronting the stillwaters trout fisherman today faced others many years ago and one of those to solve many of them was the renowned Dr H. A. Bell of Blagdon. He was sixteen when the Bristol Waterworks reservoir was first to reveal the secret of its huge trout. In the mid-thirties he had a surgery in the village, but had fished the lake for some 15 years before that and was one of the first to examine the stomach contents of the trout he caught, thus discovering that the main food of the fish consisted of small flies and aquatic creatures, nothing like the large loch and sea trout patterns generally employed by anglers in those days. From this stemmed the Worm Fly, Grenadier, Buzzer and Amber Nymph, all of which are used successfully by anglers on many stillwaters today.

Among other flies in use today solely because their worth is well proved and remains are the Black and Peacock Spider, the Cow Dung Fly, Red Tag Palmer, Soldier Palmer and Coch-y-Bondhu or other small, buzzy flies that represent a whole mass of assorted beetles and other terrestrial insects that fall from trees or are blown to the water from the moorland ling and heather and the heath grasses where they seem to swarm in summer. Cast to rising fish, even floated on spec and allowed to be carried by the wind, these land-bred creatures have become familiar to and accepted by the trout and will catch the feeding fish and often induce a take by one of those cruising several feet below the surface.

The biggish lure stripped back fast through the water that proved so effective on early visits in the first weeks of the season becomes less so now as the skilled fly fisherman begins to find increasing success with his attempts to imitate the naturals.

Already guilty of repetition of salient points in this chapter, I will stress once more the desirability of getting away from the madding crowd, even when fishing for inexperienced stockies: by doing so you will probably enjoy better sport with the smaller fish and increase the likelihood of coming across one of those big rainbows or brownies that truly make an enjoyable day a memorable one.

By seeking the open spaces you will also be able to indulge in shorter casting to undisturbed trout feeding close to the bank, stalking the rises and calculating the probable position of the cruisers before throwing your flies to that area.

But when the real heat of summer days begins to have a marked effect on the shallow water to such an extent that its temperature is unable to hold sufficient oxygen to keep the fish comfortable, then you may have to follow the rainbows to deeper parts of the lake, which probably entails hiring a boat.

Fishing from Boats

Anyone who has watched boats and boating for any length of time will appreciate that human beings are of two kinds: those who can and those who cannot adapt to the very simple demands of a boat on both boatman and passengers; the basic behaviour required of the fisherman afloat may be slightly more severe, but not enough to defeat an averagely intelligent and able-bodied being. Yet, there are some – not a few – who just cannot conform to the simplest needs for balance, stability and the lack of any sudden violent movement that can rock the boat and so send warning vibes radiating to the waiting fish.

There are bottoms that seem to become too delicate to accept a seat on hard board for more than a minute without wriggling or shifting and, while such unease can be compensated by cushions this weakness does not augur well for the expedition! Feel absolutely free to talk, to pass the coffee or sandwiches or to hand over the landing net, but do not kick the bottom boards or let an oar fall across the thwarts when you unship it. And for heaven's sake do not pick up the mud hook and cast it far into the lake like some mis-shapen Excalibur when you decide to anchor. By such actions you are also throwing away such advantages as the boat has given you!

Anyone who has drifted across still waters looking out for that rising fish will know how often a trout appears to rise within yards of the approaching boat: more often this is not a rise, but the sudden swirl of a fish until that moment quite unaware of the bulk now suddenly bearing down on it. On the whole fish like boats and will often gather in their shade at the moorings: but they do not like sudden sharp noises; they are frightened by them and sheer away from the sound waves that can travel a fair distance through water.

Incidentally, you pay good money for a boat to carry you out to where the fish are and there is absolutely no justification for standing up to cast just because by doing so you can throw a longer line. You do not have to reach the fish, the boat has done it for you and your job now is to catch them ... which you will do if you use your eyes to their maximum, your casting arm to a minimum and study to be still.

Some anglers new to the game suffer the initial illusion that because you are afloat a shorter rod and short handled landing net will suffice. Nothing could be further from the facts: for good control over line and flies, especially when fishing the drift or lock style – an increasingly popular form of fishing – the long rod is still helpful and even more so when playing a good fish around or under the boat. Also, the beaten trout can be held on the surface well away and drawn over a long handled net awaiting it below the surface. A little scoop of a net on a short handle like a ping-pong bat will require the angler or his companion to get up, lean over the gunwale or kneel on the seat to reach down to the trout.

The fisherman who cannot follow these simple guide lines might just as well save the hire charge and stay ashore: he will not catch much, maybe, but at least he will do so with less stress and discomfort.

In the early days when the West Country's new reservoirs were appearing and as boats became available to fishermen for the first time their most common use was as anchored fishing platforms and this is when you are most likely to see the occupants standing up to make their casts.

From the static boat you have arrived at where, you believe, the fish are and now you cast your lures or flies to cover an area round the boat that is within comfortable distance. Do this sitting down and you can reasonably hope that the trout will stay within range. Once I watched an angler take a boat out to a point where some very big rainbows could be seen feeding avidly on Daddies at the surface. This was on Porth reservoir before it became a coarse fishery and it was a rare opportunity to do well with the bigger trout of that lake. Alas, the angler dropped the anchor with a splash, waddled back to the centre of the boat like a duck, rocking the clinker-built craft until waves were reaching out in a widening circle around it, picked up his rod and began casting. The trout were still rising, but had edged perceptibly away from the disturbance so causing the caster to greater effort and further vibrations. He soon realised that the fish had moved beyond his reach and, after up-anchoring, was away in pursuit. The ungainly insects were still being blown to the water, the big fish were still feeding greedily but I had to watch the whole sorry exhibition of ignorance and incompetence repeated. Eventually, boat and occupant were becoming distant specks down the lake, the trout had returned to the original spot and were still rising and I rowed across to them.

It is so easy to be critical when one has enjoyed a lifetime of learning the finer points, but there are some elements in every sport that demand nothing more than a bit of thinking and commonsense.

Personally, I like to drift freely before a steady breeze and cover the water in front of me and to each side once trout are feeding in the upper layer of water. A long rod that takes a light line enables you to cast fly or team of flies gently and in the latter case to dibble the top dropper back towards you on the surface. This method provides constant action, requires constant observation and often results in a good bag of fine fish.

In a strong wind the progress of the boat may prove too fast: you find yourself bearing down on your flies much too quickly, so it is necessary to slow the rate. Oars tied to rowlocks or thole pins may work at a pinch or the anchor hanging from the bow by rope or chain, but well clear of the bottom: but there is nothing better than the purpose-built drogue. Many anglers buy these and carry them wherever they go: some fisheries provide them with the boats, but anyone can produce a makeshift drogue from a canvas bag or tough plastic sack, a bit of strong wire and light rope.

Properly positioned a drogue will not only control the pace of the drift, but the angle at which the boat is stationed across the wind. For the single angler I believe a straightforward bow into wind is best so that I can sit by the rowlocks with oars ready to hand and landing net beside me and fish over or to each side of the stern: two rods can also do this, the one closest the bow casting a fairly long line to the starboard (right) side, his companion fishing a shorter line to port (left). The onus for choosing the moment of his cast lies with the angler near the bow.

If two (or three) rods fish loch style it is necessary for their boat to drift cross-wind. Casting is reasonably short and down-wind and when drifting in this fashion it must be remembered that a fish, once hooked, should be directed round the boat so that it may be fought and netted to windward (i.e., the side towards which the wind is blowing), otherwise the boat is likely to over-run the fish as you are preparing to net it.

Loch style fly fishing has certainly become increasingly popular in recent years, especially in competitive angling: but in the West the opportunity for this is limited to a small number of the large lakes owned by water companies – Chew and Wimbleball providing two very popular venues for national and international competitions. However, drift fishing can be enjoyed on some of the smaller waters of 40 acres upwards, although some problems arise when angling shares the available space with other water sports. On some lakes where a limited number of boats is available the interests of bank fishermen, as well as others, may make boat fishing restricted to 'at anchor': indeed, as I write, boat fishing on Kennick's 45 acres is restricted in number of boats, which must be moored at certain specified points in the reservoir – again the employment of fishing platforms.

There is one other form of fly fishing from boats and that is when an experienced and competent oarsman puts the anglers in the right position and on the right course to catch their trout and maintains that happy situation, even on the smaller waters. Having mucked about in boats all my life, this is a job I personally enjoy as much, possibly even more than plying the rod! It is very rewarding ... when your efforts bring success to the rods.

12 (*above*) Stalking rising brownies in the shallows of a flooding lake.

13 (*right*) A well-dressed angler prepared to net a good brownie from Tinhays Lake at Lifton.

14 River Lyn: this Exmoor river needs rain to be at its best and provides an opportunity to fish for sea trout and salmon over six miles of the Glenthorne and Watersmeet fisheries managed by NRA South West. There are also a few privately owned stretches where day permits are available.

15 A 16 lb 9 oz pike caught at 'Claypit' ponds near Bridgwater. (*Photo: NRA*)

16 (*below*) Fishing the wet fly downstream. A guest at the Half Moon Inn fishing the river Torridge on the hotel's 5½ miles of excellently stocked brown trout fishing.

17 (*above*) Chew Valley Lake.

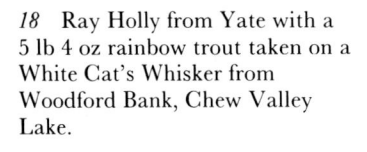

18 Ray Holly from Yate with a 5 lb 4 oz rainbow trout taken on a White Cat's Whisker from Woodford Bank, Chew Valley Lake.

5

STILLWATERS FOR TROUT

Doyen of all England's reservoir trout fisheries must be Blagdon. Born at the beginning of the century when the Bristol Waterworks Company built a dam across the river Yeo to augment their supplies to the ever-growing city, the new lake covered 440 acres at a maximum depth of 42 feet: but it is not entirely clear whether its creation of a superb trout fishery was by happy accident or as a result of the foresight of the directors of the company.

It matters not whether the first trout to indicate the incredible growth rate of fish feeding over flooding pastures were the native brownies of the little river or the imported fish from Loch Leven we know to have been introduced at some time in the early days: on visits during 1904 a handful of privileged Rods caught 102 brown trout at an average weight of almost 5 lb with the top trout weighing 9 lb 2 oz! The following season confirmed that this new-found Mecca for fishermen was no flash in the pan and an issue of the *Field* reported that two highly-respected anglers of that time, M. R. L. White and R. Hardy Corfe, fished a March Brown to land twenty fish during one day. The aggregate of this catch was over 90 lb and the biggest fish weighed $8^{1}/_{4}$ lb.

As that accomplished stillwaters fly fisherman Robin Lemon points out in *West Country Fly Fishing*, not only had the fish grown unbelievably fast on the wealth of food provided by the inundation, but there was very little rod pressure and this degree of quality could not be maintained as the reservoir settled down and access by the public became more freely available. With this in mind the company established a hatchery at the head of the lake at Ubley and this has been providing both rainbow and brown trout for the company's fisheries to this day: not only that, but Blagdon trout ova and the fish themselves have been sent to every part of the world – in 1906 to New Zealand and during the more recent past this fine stock has been used closer to home. In fact, both Siblyback Lake in Cornwall and subsequently Colliford Lake high on Bodmin Moor received the Loch Leven-Ubley strain of brownies.

This story repeated itself some fifty years later, when a similar drowning of the land took place to create the 1,200-acre reservoir now famed as Chew Valley Lake at the foot of the Mendip Hills only seven miles from Bristol.

Natural lakes and reservoirs with sufficient volume of inflowing water from streams that are home to wild brownies (and today an increaasing number of rainbows) can be self-supporting in their stocks of fish, but never on a scale needed to meet the demand for fly fishing: so, stocking with hatchery-bred and -fed fish is here to stay. The Ubley hatchery has fed Bristol fisheries at Blagdon, Chew and the little Barrow 'Tanks' over past years with enough trout to sustain an annual average Rod catch of more than 45,000 ... as well as supplying fisheries far afield.

Apart from a few days at the very start of a new season, when some popular fisheries have to limit numbers, few of the larger waters apply restrictions to numbers of fishermen: on smaller pools and lakes where stocks are excellent, but space is restricted it is obvious that only so many Rods can fish in comfort and this applies equally at those select waters where the fish are of such high quality and size that demand exceeds bank space!

Price-wise, you pay for what you may expect to receive, but some private water companies seem to offer anglers a better deal than others and get the support they fully deserve. In assessing whatever a fishery offers against the price it charges for a permit one must take into consideration not only the size and quality of the trout, the number an angler may retain and the daily catch average, but also the quality of boats where these are available, the state of the banks and paths and the amenities of club house, loos, washing facilities, shop, cafeteria etc. Not the sort of things you look for when out after wild brownies, the sea trout and salmon beside wild waters: but almost all permit fishing on stillwaters is of necessity an artificial sport and young, old or disabled, male and female, now look for such creature comforts to accompany the chance of catching trout at the price of anything between £10 and £30 per day in the 'Nineties!

In Avon county there are two other small fisheries: Church Farm at Publow, near Bristol, a 1½ acre lake fed by a spring and stocked with rainbows; and Cameley Lakes where three pools of 1, 1½ and 2 acres offer day permits for rainbows and brownies near Bristol, at Temple Cloud.

Into Somerset and you come to Wessex Water plc's trout reservoirs. In fact, you require a Wessex NRA licence to fish the Avon county waters in addition to the individual permits: on the water company's own fisheries in Somerset the licence fee is incorporated in the permit price, as, indeed, it is further west in the realm of South West Water plc. This also applies to a number of smaller, privately-owned trout stillwaters, but not at all of them and the onus is on the angler to ensure that his fishing is covered by the required licence.

Near Bridgwater are the stocked lakes of Durleigh and Hawkridge, 32 and 78 acres respectively: both offer rainbow trout with wild brownies supplemented by some stocking of reared fish. In the past Durleigh has proved one of those problem fisheries and has been closed on a number of occasions as the result of algal saturation and other problems. To the south east of Bridgwater and close to the county boundary with Dorset, at Closworth, is the 143-acre reservoir Sutton Bingham, which in the past has known problems arising from a heavy population of coarse fish, leading to turbulence and muddied waters: recently, however, the management appears to have overcome its difficulties and this is one of the better fisheries in the region and is regularly stocked with both browns and rainbows ... as is another Wessex Water fishery lying close to the county boundary with Devonshire at Clatworthy. Clatworthy of 130 acres is ex*remely popular with fly fishermen and in this rivals its larger neighbour, Wimbleball, under the ownership of South West Water: but Wessex have another little jewel in their crown –

the accent being on the 'little' referring to Otterhead Lakes near Chard. A mere 2 acres each in size with a depth of some 15 feet, two small pools constitute this picturesque fishery at the headwaters of the river Otter – as the name suggests. Stocked with rainbow trout and inhabited by wild brownies supplemented by some good reared fish the Otterhead Lakes provide sport more than commensurate with their size and the visitor should not be put off by the advice of one regular who said that if none of the locals are fishing, then it is not worthwhile a stranger doing so. As quite a number of visitors have proved the locals do not know it all! This fishery's average product over past seasons compares favourably with the rest of the Wessex Water group.

Apart from the largish waters offered by Wessex there are other privately run trouteries to the eastern side of the region – Avon Springs near Salisbury, the Cranebrook fishery at Verwood, Damerham near Fordingbridge where the big fish stalker's dream exists at Rockbourne. At Cerne Abbas are the Hermitage fishings and, near Dorchester, Flowers Farm Lakes, while back in Somerset near Somerton is Viaduct Trout fishery; at Calne in Wiltshire is Sword Lake; near Frome, St Algars Farm and, at Great Cheverill, Mill Farm Lake.

Now into the west, where South West Water plc has four important stocked fisheries, Wimbleball, Kennick & Tottiford, Siblyback and Argal Lakes, as well as the newly-styled 'budget fisheries', all but one of which are stocked with fingerlings to grow on as well as a small injection of takeable rainbow trout and for which a realistic price is levied on permits. The exception to these is 910-acre Colliford Lake on Bodmin Moor a few miles from St Neot and a bare mile from the A30 near Bolventor. Colliford has been stocked annually with 40,000 fingerlings, all of them brown trout of the old Loch Leven-Blagdon strain. It is a wild, windswept place full of trout sufficiently wild to be a challenge for even the most adept of catchers of brownies.

Colliford (almost equidistant between Launceston and Bodmin) became established as a fishery in 1986 after its creation by the South West Water Authority by flooding the little Loveney river, which becomes the St Neot and is the main tributary of the river Fowey. At that time the minor river and its head waters were a major site for the redds of spawning sea trout and to a lesser extent salmon. The loss of such a valuable breeding ground as the result of the inundation of the valley had to be compensated and the mitigation programme included the building of a hatchery below the dam where the ova from salmon and sea trout could be hatched and the small fish fed on until required for stocking. To this programme was added that of providing brown trout stock for the new reservoir and the ova for this came from brownies caught up in the feeders of nearby Siblyback Lake – descendants of the fish originally imported from the Ubley fishery at Blagdon. After the water authorities were broken into the plcs and the National Rivers Authority, the Colliford hatchery passed to the NRA SW Region: but brownies are still raised there and the lake is restocked at a rate of 40,000 fish each autumn.

The other cheaper fishing, as one might call it when permit prices are compared with those for the stocked rainbow fisheries, were originally known as natural fisheries and with the exception of the big lake on Bodmin Moor were stocked with a mixture of brownies and rainbows, providing fishing for those with shallower purses and not too much hunger for fish! However, on occasion these lakes, large and small could, can and will offer some days to remember.

Until 1990 these numbered Avon dam, Burrator, Venford, Meldon, Crowdy and Stithians and of them all the latter is known to provide some fabulous sport with wild brownies. Before Colliford arrived on the scene and prior to a worm-affliction of the trout many anglers would choose to fish Stithians rather than any of the stocked rainbow waters and there are happy indications that those days may be returning.

In 1990 such waters were re-named Budget Fisheries by South West Water plc and to their number were added Upper Tamar Lake and Wistlandpound – previously among the stocked rainbow fisheries. The fact that they had been successful stocked waters with a big following of both local and visiting Rods led to the mistake of a change in stocking policy with the corresponding result of poor sport in the first year and much complaint to the company. South West Water only needed to improve on the rate and size of the rainbows stocked to maintain some semblance of sport until the brownies put in as fingerlings had time to grow to a sporting size. I well remember SWWA wardens 'testing the waters' of Colliford with a seine net to find out whether the stock was of a size to give anglers sport before the lake was opened to fishing. That was in May and the first season at Colliford was a short one, opening on 13 July and closing on 13 October.

That netting revealed that natural fish already in the Loveney when they 'put the plug in' had also benefited from the rich feeding provided by the flood and some very fine fish were revealed then: even more so when we inspected the traps set in the feeders to pick up trout ripe for stripping at the hatchery; but among the fish caught in the seine were some fine sea trout smolts, ready to go to sea, but landlocked. Of course, the flooding began in July and sea trout were freshly arrived in the stream, while the progeny of the previous two winters were still there. Some good sea trout were caught on fly that season and fish still turn up in the spring dressed in the sea-going livery of the peal!

Of South West Water's 'Top Four', Wimbleball Lake is the largest at 374 acres and the newest, having opened to anglers in 1980. The previous year SWWA held a press preview and to those of us fortunate to attend and sample the fishing it was obvious that this was expected to be the market leader among stillwater fisheries in the authority's region. That first season saw more than 27,000 trout weighed-in by the Rods, the biggest a rainbow of 6 lb 10 oz that had grown on from one of the 5 to 6 inch fish initially put into the lake.

Following that earlier flooding to create a reservoir at Blagdon ninety years ago it seems that we still expect the end-product to produce monster brown trout. It was not the case at Wimbleball, although huge trout are still believed to swim the deeps, in fact they are known to do so and have in several cases smashed the light tackle the modern angler chooses to use – indeed, is required to do so if he wishes to score consistently. And the younger purely brown trout fishery at Colliford has yet to see landed one of the huge trout we know to be there. Wimbleball has given some very fine sport to thousands of fly-fishermen and still gives up some 16,000 trout each year at a rod/day average of 2.5 or better.

Wimbleball is situated on Exmoor a few miles from Dulverton and only a short distance from Wessex Water's Clatworthy to the east: the two lakes offer a pleasant variety of sport to anyone visiting the area.

The Kennick fishing is close to Hennock, near Bovey Tracey and used to comprise the three comparatively small reservoirs of Kennick, Tottisford and Trenchford. The latter is now one of the few pike fisheries in Devon, but Kennick of 45 acres and the slightly smaller Tottisford are very popular and, for their size, give a remarkable return approaching 10,000 fish in a season at an average of a brace per Rod. Unfortunately, this is one of those fisheries recently plagued by the potentially toxic blue green algae at times of heat and drought and was closed to fishing in 1989 and 1990. Time may find the answer to this problem, but until the solution is discovered Kennick will continue to be at risk – with a good many other unfortunates – when similar conditions prevail.

West of these lakes and high on Dartmoor on the head waters of the river Teign, near Chagford, lies Fernworthy. For some years this was stocked with both brown and rainbow trout by the water authority, but annually there was a big problem with the pH of the water in spring, sometimes producing heavy and costly loss among stock fish. It was always a month later opening for fishing and still is, but today it is a fishery stocked with brown trout. It has given up brownies in excess of 6 lb, but with a rod catch average of about 1.7 is expensive, although brown trout fishing seems to command an increasing premium these days: but I believe those lakes where the browns grow on naturally from fry and fingerling stocking consistently offer a better chance of sport, although neither on those wild waters or on those stocked with big browns is a fish guaranteed, whatever the permit costs!

To reach the company's next stocked rainbow lakes we must travel into Cornwall, where close to Colliford is Siblyback Lake, near the village of St Cleer and only a few miles from the town of Liskeard. This 140-acre reservoir was first a brown trout fishery after an initial stocking with the Loch Leven-Blagdon fish already referred to. This was in the days of the old East Cornwall Water Co., but when SWWA took over in 1974 the lake was one of those heavily stocked with rainbow trout. Others were Kennick, Upper Tamar, Argal and Porth (now a coarse fishery). In those early days there was just one massive injection of hitherto alien fish and the local Rods were exultant in the first weeks, enthusiasm dwindling as the stock was reduced and no replacements were forthcoming.

Few fishery managements steer their way through recurring seasons without a fair share of headaches: but experience, though hard, is a pretty thorough taskmaster and SWWA did not repeat the mistake. In one form or another trickle-stocking based on catch returns in part and an agreed stocking rate in the main ensures trout for fishermen throughout the season. Fish management and the care of rainbows in holding cages has improved greatly during the past decade and the days are hopefully gone when a successful fly-fisherman gazed on the wretched three-quarter pound rainbow stockie lying in his net – slimy, thin, tail rotted away and often one fin or another missing. I returned a lot of fish like that at one period and cured my own revulsion by not fishing that water again until many, many moons had passed.

As the well-established reputation of Chew Valley Lakes and more recently that of Wimbleball draw anglers from far afield, the patronage of Kennick is aided by the angling potential from Exeter and district, that of Siblyback Lake from an area including Tavistock and Plymouth as well as the smaller Cornish towns, while in the far west Argal Lake draws on Falmouth, Truro and Penzance districts and to all these populations are added the summer visitors. With fishing allowed from one hour before dawn to an hour after sunset the holidaying paterfamilias with a yearning to fish can usually find time to look after his family and enjoy some hours with the fly rod – often at times, mark you, when in a hot July or August the trout are most likely to oblige him!

Recently and during the hot spells of the 'eighties Siblyback Lake escaped the pestilential infestations of algae experienced on smaller waters. It is a good lake to fish and gives an annual return of about 7,000 with an average close on a brace per Rod – an average which would be considerably greater should the better conditions for fishing occur over longer periods.

During the reign of the South West Water Authority Argal was a highly popular stocked rainbow fishery, providing fishing for anglers in boats or along the banks around its 65 acres. With the advent of the new water company it remained one of the top stocked fisheries, but a new rule was introduced limiting fishing to boat anglers only – the reason offered being the right of others to enjoy the amenity offered by a walk along its banks. Strong intervention by the local angling club CAST with the support of the local Member of Parliament and a number of councils enable fly-fishermen to enjoy the banks through the first two months of the season, but from June 1 the boat rule applied with the result that the total number of Rods fishing the lake each week fell to less than forty on occasions. This limited few who could afford the price of both fishing and boat permit not unreasonably enjoyed some excellent fishing while a great many more had to seek other outlets.

Whether or not the figures for the season as a whole will cause second thoughts for the water company on the future management of Argal remains to be seen but it is a fishery that has been enjoyed by many in the past and it will be a shame if its facilities are limited to a few with money to spare in the future!

Another 65-acre lake, Drift, lies to the west of Penzance and brings us to the review of fisheries in Cornwall, Devon and West Somerset not owned by South West Water. Day permits are available from the fishing warden nearby and – as with all fisheries in this book – details are given at the end of the chapter. This lake is well-established and stocked with rainbows and browns, some attaining a good size. It is one of the privately owned waters where the NRA licence is required as well as a fishing permit but at many of the smaller waters the management take out a block licence; where possible such information is included with details of permits etc, although, of course, many of the rules governing fisheries may well alter from season to season.

A few miles out of Truro at St Allen is a 1½-acre lake known as Gwarnick Mill, where a modest price is levied for the fishing plus a charge per pound for the trout. It is a very pleasant fishery, well stocked and open through the year.

Retracing our steps along the main highway spine through Cornwall and Devon to the M5 – the A30 – a detour towards St Austell takes you to Innis Moor and the splendid fly fishery that saw its origin in the dreams of a clay miner's son. Three lakes totalling 6 acres and fed by a stream in the heart of the mining country are extremely well stocked and managed, providing easy access to clear banks in an unspoilt landscape with the added facilities of a comfortable club house, bar, pool room, restaurant and accommodation if needed. The original trout pond was dug from a piece of wilderness ground and covered a bare half acre: but was soon followed by another of 1½ acres and a few years later a larger lake of 4 acres on which a boat is available. The fishery, which supplies markets with trout for the table, rears all its fish and only stocks with female rainbows and triploids to enable fishing to continue throughout the winter months.

Continuing eastwards the A30 takes you past the turning to Colliford Lake and on to Five Lanes, where the turning to Camelford will lead you through the village of Altarnun where there is a pleasant little fishery comprising two small inter-linking pools of a total of 2 acres known as Rose Park and stocked with rainbow trout in excess of 2 lb, some fish attaining 5 lb and more. The road to Camelford leads to Davidstow Moor and the Budget Fishery of Crowdy reservoir and so to Camelford and another small fishery.

Again on the A30, crossing the county boundary into Devon you come to the village of Lifton and the Arundell Arms Hotel where occasional tickets can be had to fish the small, but picturesque Tinhays Lake – a flooded quarry containing some fine brown trout and rainbows. If hotel guests are not booked on the water, the visitor may be able to purchase a permit. The water is deep and clear and the trout can prove difficult, but are well-worth the catching! The Arundell Arms features significantly in our sections on river game fishing.

As you cross into Devon the peninsula broadens considerably between Hartland Point on the north coast near Bude and Start Point in the south and the A30 trunk road as a main access to the fisheries no longer remains the only one: the A39 is a northern route from Wadebridge, through Bude, Bideford and Barnstaple where it leads to Exmoor, Minehead and a union with the M5 at Bridgwater. In the south the A38 leaves the A30 at Bodmin and runs through Liskeard to Plymouth, thence to Exeter where it links with the M5 but proceeds eastwards through Honiton, Yeovil and Salisbury.

This southern route takes the angler close to both Colliford and Siblyback Lakes near Liskeard and, some seven miles north of Plymouth, the Budget fishery of Burrator – a delightfully picturesque water – is situated just east of Yelverton, while a little further along the A38 is Ivybridge and close-by Ermington where there is the small fly-only trout fishery at Mill Leat Trout Farm. From here it is a matter of joining the B3207 at Modbury and so on to Gara Bridge and the Newhouse Farm fishing on a four acre lake containing both rainbow trout and brownies. Self-catering accommodation is also available. The fishing is by fly only and rainbows to almost 14 lb have been taken.

The A38, however, continues to South Brent about four miles south of the moorland reservoir known as Avon Dam, where fishing for brown trout with fly and bait is available, but entails a walk of about 1^1/$_2$ miles from Shipley Bridge car park, unless special arrangement is made for the disabled. Information on this should be sought from South West Water. Further along the road at Ashburton the road through Holne leads on to another moorland water of about 33 acres known as Venford which provides brown trout fishing for anglers spinning or using 'bubble-float' fly fishing. As on all waters an NRA licence is required, but fishing has hitherto been free.

A few miles east of Ashburton the road crosses the A382 which leads north to Moretonhampstead. At Bovey Tracey the turning to Hennock continues on to three South West Water reservoirs – top stocked trout fisheries of Kennick and Tottiford, 45 and 35 acres respectively, and Trenchford which is now a pike fishery. Kennick is a popular venue for fly fishers, local and visitor alike: unfortunately in 1989 and 1990 occurrences of potentially toxic blue-green algae forced a cessation of fishing over fairly long periods. On to Moretonhampstead and to Chagford, where, high in the moor, lies Fernworthy – a 76-acre reservoir and stocked brown trout water belonging to South West Water. Chagford is just as easily reached from the A30 at Whiddon Down but the main southern route continues to Chudleigh and Watercress Farm, where three lakes offer excellent fly fishing for rainbows.

Beyond Exeter, close to Honiton is Hollies Trout Farm at Sheldon, where fly fishing for rainbows is available on a 1^1/$_2$ acre pond.

Returning to the northern road at Bude there is the 81-acre Upper Tamar Lake about five miles north of the coastal town and about two miles east of Kilkhampton. Now one of the SWW budget fisheries, Upper Tamar was through the eighties one of the most popular fly fishing stillwaters in Devon and Cornwall. Its beginning as a trout fishery stocked with fry in 1990 was not a success, but it may well develop into a rewarding lake and a very pleasant one to fish.

And on up to Bideford where the two four acre lakes forming Gammaton reservoirs have been stocked and managed by the Torridge Fly Fishing Club who issue day permits; the future of this fishing is, unfortunately, not certain at the time of writing. Another lake called Melbury and covering 12 acres was also run by another club, but in 1990 was taken back by the water company and turned to coarse fishing.

At the other end of the joint estuary of rivers Torridge and Taw is Barnstaple and near it at Muddiford are the Blakewell Fisheries comprising lakes of one and four acres stocked with both brownies and rainbows. Not far away is Wistlandpound, another SWW budget fishery that has to develop from its original status of first a rainbow trout water, then a stocked brown trout lake.

About half way along the A39 from Barnstaple to Lynton you come to Blackmoor Gate. There is a public house by the crossroads and, taking the road leading to South Molton the next turning right leads to this 41-acre fishery in most attractive surroundings. From Blackmoor Gate, too, the B3358 takes you into the heart of Exmoor to link up with the B3223 at Simonsbath and so to Winsford Hill and into the valley of the Barle and the Somerset town of Dulverton. A mere matter of minutes and you reach Exbridge and the A396 running through the edge of the beautiful Brendon Hills to Dunster. But pause at Exbridge where there are two permit fisheries – Lakeside, stocked with rainbows, and two small lakes run by the Exe Valley Fishery. The former is run by John Sharpe, who can also provide river trouting and salmon fishing on the local streams. But here we are within six miles of Wimbleball Lake – probably one of the most consistently rewarding stocked trout waters in the West.

Even the most amateur reader of maps will appreciate that this tour of the western side of our region has brought us back to the vicinity of that artery of road travel, the M5. From it at Bridgwater and Taunton the A39 and A358 run along each side of the Quantock Hills to join at Williton and run on westwards along the coast to Dunster, Minehead, up Porlock Hill and along the northern edge of Exmoor until the A39 arrives at Lynton, more or less where we left it.

But back to Launceston, the A30 and a more central return to the M5. Just outside Launceston, close to St Giles on the Heath at Sitcott, beside the river Carey, there was a popular trout fly fishing water started by Mike Summers of The Angling Centre at Launceston. The future of this water – closed during 1990 – is not known: but potentially it could again be a fishery and is worth making an inquiry. Once again, the best place to inquire is at the Angling Centre referred to and also all tackle shops and licence agents for any new fisheries in their areas.

Beyond the village of Lifton on the A30 the main roads leads on to Okehampton where Meldon reservoir's 54 acres lie close to the great rock quarry where ravens nest. These birds are important because they are said to restock those at the Tower of London, without which England will fall! The fishery itself has hitherto proved of little account and is free to anglers possessing a trout licence. However, before it reaches Okehampton the road passes a turning to Bratton Clovelly and leads to South Reed Fisheries. Situated in a nature reserve this includes a $4^1/_2$-acre trout lake for the fly only.

This area, however, holds a very big secret – one yet to be revealed in detail. After years of argument and counter-argument between conservationists and those with a duty to provide water to a drought-ridden area of the South West, approval was granted the South West Authority to build a large supply reservoir on the course of the river Wolf, which is one of the Tamar's tributaries. This has been known as Roadford and, at the time of writing, it is about to come on stream. Already its swelling waters are being claimed as a haven for water fowl and it is understood that Roadford will join Colliford in the category of National Brown Trout fishery in 1993.

Another road from Launceston runs north to Holsworthy, where the Mill Leat fishery is situated at Thornbury then east to Hatherley. Some three miles before reaching the latter town is a cross roads and the hamlet of Highamton and the site of popular trout fishery. From Hatherley the A386 leads northwards to Huish – about five miles – just before which a turning to the right will take the angler to Dolton, close by which is the well-known Stafford Moor fishery with two lakes of 14 and 7 acres. Hitherto this water has enjoyed a fine reputation despite many vicissitudes sent to try owner and management. For several years it has been the venue for the final of the Television South West individual fly fishing championships, attracting many of the best competition fishermen from all parts of the region after the qualifying heats held at other fisheries in Cornwall, Devon and Somerset. And so we go on our way via Crediton to Tiverton, where the six pools of the Bellbrook Valley Fishery offer sport with the fly throughout the year. This water actually lies about seven miles from the town and about two miles from Oakford village, near Bampton, and can be reached from either the A361 or B3221. And once you are there it is only a step or so to Exebridge and a few miles from the M5. Our tour of the stillwater fly fishing is complete.

Stillwater Trout Fisheries
(other than those managed by Water Companies and detailed in Appendix 5)

WESSEX REGION

Avon Area

Cameley Lakes
Hillcrest Farm, Cameley,
Temple Cloud, Bristol
Tel: Temple Cloud 52423

Church Farm
Publow, Pensford, Nr Bristol
Tel: Compton Dando 231

Somerset Area

St Algars Farm
West Woodlands, Frome
Tel: Maiden Bradley 233

Sword Lake
Quemerford Gate Farm,
Cherhil Nr Calne
Tel: Calne 812388

Viaduct Fishery
Cary Valley, Somerton

Avon & Dorset Area

Avon Springs
Recreation Road, Durrington
Walls, Salisbury
Tel: Durrington Walls 53557

Cranebrook Fishery
Verwood, West Quay Road,
Poole
Tel: Poole 680462

Damerham Fisheries Ltd
Fordingbridge
Hants
Tel: Rockbourne 446

Dorset Springs
Poole Road, Sturminster
Marshall, Dorset
Tel: Sturminster Marshall
857653

Flowers Farm Fishery
Hilfield, Dorchester, Dorset
Tel: Cerne Abbas 351

Hermitage Fishing Lakes
Cerne Abbas, Dorset
Tel: Holnest 556

Knights in the Bottom
Fishery
Hooke, Beaminster, Dorset

Langford Fishery
Steeple Langford, Salisbury,
Wilts

Mangerton Lake
Bridport, Dorset

Mill Farm Lake
Great Cheverell, Devizes
Wilts
Tel: Devizes 813325

Myrtle Farm Fishery
Waytown, Bridport, Dorset

Pallington Lakes
Tingleton, Dorchester,
Dorset
Tel: Puddletown 8141

STILLWATERS FOR TROUT

Rawlsbury Waters
Higher Ansty, Dorset

Rockbourne Fisheries Ltd
Sandleheath, Fordingbridge
Tel: Rockbourne 603

Tolpuddle Fishery
Lawrence's Farm,
Tolpuddle, Dorchester
Tel: Puddletown 8460

Walden's
Crockford Road, West
Grimstead, Salisbury, Wilts
Tel: 710480

Whitesheet Fishery
Holt, Wimborne, Dorset
Tel: Wimborne 842772

Zeals Fishery
Green Stones, Wolverton,
Zeals, Warminster
Tel: Bourton 840573

SOUTH WEST REGION
Cornwall

Fenwick Fishery
Dunmere Bridge, Bodmin
Tel: Bodmin 78296

Gwarnick Mill
St Allen, nr Truro
Tel: Zelah 487

Innis Farm
Innis Moor, Penwithick,
St Austell
Tel: St Austell 851162

Lake View Country Club
Lanivet, Bodmin
Tel: Lanivet 831808

Rose Park Fishery
Trezibbet, Altarnun,
Launceston
Tel: Pipers Pool 86278

Devon

Bellbrook Valley
Oakford, Tiverton
Tel: Oakford 292

Blakewell Fisheries
Muddiford, Barnstaple
Tel: Barnstaple 44533

Gammaton Reservoirs
Bideford (Torridge FFC)
Tel: Bideford 77980
or day permits from The
Tackle Shop in Bideford

Hartsbeer Lake
Goodalls Farm, Hemyock,
Nr Cullompton
Tel: Hemyock 680319

Hollies Farm
Sheldon, Honiton
Tel: Broadhembury 428

Mill Leat
Thornbury, Holsworthy
Tel: Holsworthy 26426

Newhouse Fishery
Moreleigh, Totnes
Tel: Gara Bridge 426

South Reed Fishery
Bratton Clovelly,
Okehampton
Tel: Bratton Clovelly 295

Stafford Moor
Brightley Barton, Dolton,
Winkleigh
Tel: Dolton 360

Stout Fishery
Billingsmoor, Butterleigh,
Cullompton
Tel: Cullompton 248

Watercress Farm
Kerswell Springs, Chudleigh
Tel: Chudleigh 852168

Somerset

Exe Valley Fishery
Exebridge, Dulverton
Tel: Dulverton 23328

Lakeside
Parlour Cottage, Higher
Grants, Exebridge
Tel: Dulverton 23104

THE COTSWOLDS

Horseshoe Lake
Wildmoorway Lane, South
Cerney
Tel: Cirencester 861006

Lechlade Trout Farm
Burford Road, Lechlade
Tel: Lechlade 53266

6

COARSE FISHING AND FISHERIES

Coarse fishing in the West Country has existed as long as the rivers have drained the wetlands, flowed down from the limestone of the Cotswolds or the chalk of the Wiltshire plains to culminate in the Bristol Channel or the English one. Even before the rod and line gave a sporting emphasis to the effort, early men sought sustenance from the rivers and took eels, pike, bream and roach in traps of local withies, nets of coarse thread and by means of barbed spears and forks. The sport, however, grew just as it did elsewhere throughout central and southern England, apart from in the far west, where the slightly acid waters and nature of the spate rivers did little to comfort the so-called coarse members of the tribe, but welcomed the returning migratory salmon and trout and maintained fine stocks of healthy, indigenous brownies.

That is now changed and the recent past has seen a sudden provision of opportunities to catch most of those that do not carry the hallmark of the game fish – the fleshy adipose fin or posterior dorsal that marks salmon, trout and grayling, as well as the chars and white fish. As a mere lad of some ten years I would have told you that there was no fishing to be had at all in Cornwall, except in the seas around the Peninsula. You see I was then a coarse fisherman and I wanted to catch coarse fish and there were none. Today the scene has changed and there is fishing to be had of this kind ... almost to the end of the land itself!

But, almost for the first time in this book, I have mentioned grayling. This is the odd fish out, as it were. Neither fish, nor fowl, nor ... it carries that adipose fin – hallmark of the aristocrat – yet it is treated as a coarse fish and almost with contempt, even in those areas where it provides fly fishing after the brown trout have moved away to the spawning gravels and grows to a size that compares very favourably with the norm of the wild brownie. Even in Cornwall the grayling frequents the Tamar and its tributaries and on the upper Inny reaches weights close on two pounds: but it is a fish of fastidious taste for water purity and cannot be relied on in our rivers as they are today. The tale is different to the east where the chalk streams offer it more acceptable conditions, but where man sometimes does not welcome it sharing with his precious trout! Maybe a wild brownie is superior as a quarry, but faced with the choice between a stew-fed trout, brown or rainbow, I will choose the grayling every time. However, good grayling fishing is harder to find in the south west than sport with trout.

Pike fishing, too, is not commonly to be had in Devon and none exists in Cornwall where the fish itself, *Esox lucius*, has never been known. South West Water's Peninsula Coarse Fisheries does stock Trenchford reservoir, near Bovey Tracey and close to the trout fishery at Kennick, with pike up to 30 lbs, but it is really as artificial as the stocked rainbows that provide fly-fishermen with their sport on the neighbouring water: there are few natural quarry for the pike to eat, but anglers may catch these fish on spinners, spoons and plugs, earthworms (not a particularly popular bait) or dead sea fish. The other venue available is at the nature reservoir at Slapton Ley, where pike to 20 lb are caught by spinning or the use of dead sea fish. Other possibilities are the Grand Western Canal at Tiverton and a six miles length of the Exeter Canal.

In general almost all the coarse fishing in this western area is confined to stillwaters from the smallest of ponds to large waters like SWW plc's reservoirs at Porth, Lower Tamar and College – each about 40 acres and containing carp, tench, bream, roach and rudd, the accent being on the first three which produce specimen fish each season. In fact, carp and tench really predominate at almost all stillwater fisheries throughout the west area.

In the Wessex area, however, pike are more frequently found in both rivers and lakes, the grayling is a worthy quarry on the few rivers where fishing is available to the visitor and common species are roach and bream, with dace and chub occurring where conditions suit them, which also applies to carp and tench. Pike and perch are somewhat localised and the barbel – virtually a newcomer to the west of the area – at the moment is only found in the Bristol Avon system – but is, of course, one of the fish that has made the Hampshire Avon at Christchurch famous, also the lower reaches of the Dorset Stour.

The variety of fishing is equalled by the methods which can prove successful. The usual mass of baits in every shape, guise and colour (maggots and boilies stained all the colours of the rainbow and more besides) can be offered to the fish in divers ways. It attracts the specimen hunter and the match fisherman, as well as that not inconsiderable contingent who fish for the pure pleasure of doing so. As a boy I watched the last of the great roach-pole fishermen on the river Lea in Hertfordshire: they died out as did those long bamboo poles with their sensitive tips; but now the modern poler can be seen in the West and the rod he uses is longer by far than those of his predecesors ... thanks to the arrival of graphite! Others use more conventional tackle either lying-on for the bottom feeders or fishing the stream for roach and dace or long-trotting for chub as one would for sea trout or grayling, using maggots or small and lively redworms. Some use a static ledger. Some spin, some fly fish.

It seems hardly necessary to point out that an NRA licence is essential before you start to fish ... even on the most private ponds: but a season licence for coarse fish may cost no more than the day permit to fish and licences to cover a week can also be had. Here once again the local tackle dealer comes to the fore: he will almost certainly be a distributor for the NRA and an agent for any permit fisheries in the area. If, in fact, he is unable to supply you he will be able to direct you to the person who can. At the same time, he will be able to supply any equipment you may need, advise on local methods and baits and probably supply some of the baits you may need. For years past the popular maggot was in very short supply, a rarity indeed in the far west. There was little demand for it, but this changed as coarse fishing developed and tackle dealers found themselves stocking rods never known before, ground-bait dispensers, floats and other unfamiliar items including keep-nets.

Keep-nets are, of course, indispensable for fishing contests, but I personally do not find much sense in confining your captives during the hours of fishing in order to release them at the end of the day. The latest nets are designed to do as little as possible to the scaly flanks of fish, but it is difficult to assess just how effective they actually are in doing so and one of the problems of returning the catch to the water is the danger that some unnoticeable damage has been done which can lead to infection by parasites who start a disease that is transmissible.

On the other hand, it is understandable that an angler may wish to be able to admire, even show it off to others at the end of the day. The dangers stemming from the use of keep-nets is greater when the temperature of stillwaters is at its highest in the summer. Often you will see the net suspended in the shallowest water, sometimes collapsed on its occupants and that cannot be right. I will always remember the end of the Big'un – the huge contest held annually by Birmingham Anglers Association on the rivers Severn and Avon. That year the winner was pegged on what is known as the Mill Avon at Tewkesbury where he fished brilliantly among great shoals of bleak and won the competition with a catch that numbered in hundreds, getting closer to the thousand than mattered much. I recall that at least three long match nets were used, but at the end of it all, after the weighing, the catch was returned to the river where its shining silvery little components floated upside down towards the sea, white bellies looking like a shower of confetti or a fall of blossom. Care should be taken over the quality of the nets used for landing fish, especially big fellows like carp, which must be returned to the water as soon as landed at most fisheries.

It is of interest, I think, that National Rivers Authority bye-laws ban the transfer of fish from any one water to another, river or lake, and it seems more than likely that the use of barbless hooks for coarse fishing will become mandatory at an increasing number of fisheries. This rule is now accepted at all catch-and-return trout waters and logic would suggest that it should also apply to all coarse fisheries where the catch must be returned at the end of fishing. I have been told by many anglers with greater experience of using these hooks than I that relatively few fish are lost during the fight to bring them to the landing net: my own limited experience, however, gives the lie to this where such lively or tricky fighters as grayling and sea trout are concerned. But, in any case, why worry about losing the odd fish if you are going to put it back anyway?

At this point anglers with experiences of shoal fish like perch (especially perch), roach, tench and barbel, also grayling and school peal will tell you that a fish that has been hooked and lost will immediately communicate with its brethren, after which no further bites will be forthcoming for some considerable time. My own experiences give such statements support and I have been convinced by studies of rainbow trout at somewhat restricted fisheries that communications between individual fish and the shoal do exist, even to the extent that trout pricked by one pattern of fly will promptly warn the others not to touch that said offering!

It is for this reason that some anglers defend their use of the keep-net, yet, I just wonder whether the presence of such a 'prison' and the unfortunates it incarcerates is not itself a warning 'pour encourager les autres' – just as prison is intended to be?

Some fisheries also apply restrictions to methods of fishing and to baits, while the use of cereal ground baits in bulk is banned at all supply reservoirs and many other smaller waters. The judicious use of cereals as a form of packing in bait dispensers, however, is accepted in most places and the use of broadcast bait – usually the hook bait of maggot, stewed wheat, bread pellets, sweet corn, worms, cheese etc is permitted.

On baits, one final point: you are advised to bring your own worms with you as well as fancifully coloured maggots and home-made boilies ... or the means to colour them.

In the following pages a review of rivers and stillwaters available for coarse fishing will name such angling clubs controlling the fisheries and, as already suggested, permits will usually be obtainable from tacklists or licence distributors in nearby towns. However, this is not always the case and so far as stillwaters are concerned most of the large lakes and reservoirs have their own self-service units or issue permits through nearby cottage or farmhouse.

A new feature introduced this season by Peninsula Coarse Fisheries is the application of Castabout permits. These enable the angler to fish a number of reservoirs on the same permit and are available for the season at the larger lakes while a seven day Castabout is offered to cover some of the smaller fisheries as well. The latter, I am sure, will be of great interest to holiday fishermen. Details appear later in the review.

As already explained, the Wessex region of the National Rivers Authority is both operationally and administratively divided into three areas – the first based on the watershed of the Bristol Avon, secondly the area to the east, known as the Avon & Dorset area, bounded by that other Avon that rises in Wiltshire and runs down to join the sea near Christchurch and is famed by the name of Hampshire Avon. Finally, the Somerset area, which includes the rivers rising from the eastern edge of Exmoor, the Quantocks and the Brendon hills as well as the popular coarse fisheries of the rivers and drains of the Somerset Levels.

Bristol Avon Area

Obviously, having given its name to the area the river Avon is the main river from its headwaters in the Cotswolds at Tetbury, Didmarton and Badminton to its tidal reach that begins at Keynsham Weir and ends in the Severn estuary, but it has many important tributaries including the river Frome, the Boyd, By Brook, Semington and Midford brooks and rivers Marden, Somerset Frome, Biss and Chew. From the City of Bristol (where fishing is available in the docks and Floating Harbour), circling clockwise, the area encompasses Malmesbury, Calne and Chippenham, Melksham and Devizes, Trowbridge, Frome, Radstock and Bath in the centre.

Another useful but variable fishery of considerable length is the Kennet and Avon Canal linking the Bristol Avon to the Kennet in Berkshire, extending from Bath to a point near Reading. These waters afford the angler with a wide range of species including roach, dace, chub, bream, perch, pike and barbel in certain reaches: also trout and grayling, but the streams providing the best of the game fishing are strictly preserved and are unlikely to be available to the visiting angler.

However, fishing rights to many miles on most of the main river and tributaries are enjoyed by a large number of clubs and permits can be obtained to fish most of them. The headwaters of the main river join forces at Malmesbury, where free fishing is to be had at the recreation ground, below which the coarse fishing improves and the waters are swelled by the Woodbridge Brook and Brinkworth Brook. Somerfords FA controls a good length of river in this section.

So on downstream to Chippenham where, again, there is some free fishing, but the river above is controlled mainly by Isis AC and Chippenham AA. From here to Staverton the Avon meanders through a delightful pastoral setting, through a wide plain, and offers sport with bream, carp, chub, dace, eels, perch, pike, roach, tench and trout and small lengths are available to the permit-holder, but at Melksham drainage work has made the river deeper and wider. In this area and downriver to Bradford-on-Avon the river is swelled by the river Marden from Calne and the Semington Brook and the fishing is controlled by Melksham & District AA and Bradford-on-Avon & District AA with some smaller stretches of river available to visitors on waters of the Portcullis AA and Silver Dace AA.

We now approach the new barbel fisheries, where this fish was introduced to the river at Bathampton, Claverton and Limpley Stoke from the mid-fifties. There is some free fishing in this area, while a large stretch is controlled by Bathampton AA and other smaller reaches by Silver Dace, Bath, Bristol Golden Carp and Avon Tributaries associations.

The strange character of this river is the way it runs southwards from its sources, skirting the Cotswold foothills, to level out on an east west axis briefly after Melksham only to rise sharply northwards to Bath, where it is joined by the By Brook, then runs westwards to Bristol and the Channel beyond, taking in the river Boyd, the Somerset Frome, the Chew and the Bristol Frome. As a watershed it can claim a mass of smaller and larger feeder streams, all of which contain fish from trout and grayling to gudgeon and 'Daddy' ruffes.

From Bath the fishable waters are managed variously (and in small sections) by Arrowsmiths, City of Bristol, Bristol & West of England Anglers Federation, Portcullis, Stapleton, Mardon and Keynsham fishing associations. It is at Keynsham that the Avon begins to feel the effect of the spring tides from the Channel and at Netham the river splits, providing water for the Bristol docks, while the other branch becomes much affected by the tides and flounders may well contribute to a mixed bag including some fine bream. However, within the city there is increased fishing in the docks and harbour and enquiries should be made to the

Baltic Wharf Leisure Centre, Bristol or to Bristol & West of England Federation of Anglers.

It is in the heart of Bristol that the river Frome joins the major river after travelling a far shorter distance along the western edge of the hills from a source at Dodington, not far from the western beginning of the Avon itself.

Tributaries
Bristol Frome
Somerfords FA, Frome Vale FA, Bristol Omnibus FA, Bristol City Council.
Bream, carp, dace, eel, perch, roach, tench and trout.

River Boyd (also rises close to Dodington, joining main river at Bitton)
Adult Schools AA and Portcullis AA have small stretches: Golden Valley FC has a bigger water close to Bristol.
Bream, crucian carp, dace, eel, gudgeon, perch, roach and trout.

By Brook (formed by Broadmead Brook and Burton Stream, flows through Castle Combe and enters Avon at Bathford)
Strictly preserved for trout through much of length. Coarse fishing for dace and roach in lower reaches through Bathampton AA.

River Marden (springs from Marlborough Downs to join main river above Chippenham)
Much of river a trout stream, but below Calne coarse fish take over and barbel, too, may be found close to the junction with the Avon. Isis AC control a section, but a larger stretch is held by Calne AA.
Barbel, chub, dace, pike, perch, roach and trout.

Semington Brook (fed from Salisbury Plain it joins Avon below Melksham)
Holds brown trout in upper reaches, but coarse fish prevail in the lower stream and fishing is managed by Bradford-on-Avon AA.
Bream, chub, dace, eel, perch, pike, roach, tench and trout.

River Biss (joins Avon at Trowbridge)
Hardly worth bothering about.

Midford Brook (includes Wellow and Cam Brooks, rising on the Mendip Hills but polluted by mining for much of its existence)
High quality trout fishing has been developed by controlling clubs, but coarse fishing is limited to the low reaches where barbel, dace, roach and trout can be found. Not worth considering by visitors.

River Chew (rises near Chewton Magna, feeds Bristol Waterworks Co. prestige Chew Valley trout fishery and continues to Keynsham to join the Avon)
A popular coarse fishery with free fishing for juniors along the footpath at Keynsham: otherwise controlled by a number of angling clubs including Knowle AA, Bristol Golden Carp AA, Chew Fly Fishing Club, Silver Dace AA, City of Bristol AA and Keynsham AA.
Bream, dace, eel, grayling, perch, roach, tench and trout.

Somerset Frome (main tributary of the Avon it draws its water from the limestone and chalk of the Mendips and around Warminster and joins the main river west of Trowbridge).
The headwaters and tributaries provide excellent conditions for trout fishing, but the lower river from Frome to its junction with the Avon is an important and interesting coarse fishery. Permits are available through the Frome & District AA.

Although the secretaries of angling clubs change with the passing seasons, their addresses will usually lead to enquiries being passed on to the new officer and we add this list, updated so far as is possible. Also, there is a list of private stillwaters coarse fisheries in the Bristol Avon area and a note of such free fishing as is available as well as facilities for disabled anglers.

ANGLING CLUB SECRETARIES

Alcove Lido AC
R. C. Hole, 70 Pound Road, Bristol
Fishponds Lido (Bristol), River Chew

Avon AC (Melksham)
R. Edwards, 56 Addisar Road, Melksham
Tel: 705036
Avon (Melksham)

Avon FFC
S. Filton, 39 Fouracres Close, Withywood, Bristol

Avon and Tributaries AA
J. G. Lewis, Chapel Cottage, Clarendon Road, Widcombe, Bath
Tel: Bath 20089
Avon, Frome (Somerset), Cam Brook, Wellow Brook, Midford Brook

Avon Preservation and Restocking Society
C. D. Wiltshire, Lark Rise, Main Road, Temple Cloud, Bristol
Tel: Temple Cloud 52872

Bath AA
A. J. Smith, 68 Bloomfield Rise, Odd Down, Bath
(Refer to Bristol, Bath and Wiltshire Amalgamated Anglers)
Tel: Bath 834736
Avon, Cam Brook, Wellow Brook, Willow Lake (Westbury), Burton Hill Lake (Malmesbury)

Bathampton AA
D. Crookes, 25 Otago Terrace, Larkhall, Bath
Tel: Bath 27164

Avon, By-Brook, Wellow Brook, Kennet & Avon Canal, Woodborough Lake (Peasedown), Hunstrete Lake (Marksbury)

Bradford-on-Avon District AA
M. Harding, 9 Grosvenor Villas, Claremont Road, Larkhall, Bath
Tel: 445832
Avon, Semington Brook, Frome, (Somerset), Kennet & Avon Canal

Bristol, Bath and Wiltshire Amalgamated Anglers
J. S. Parker, 16 Lansdown View, Kingswood, Bristol
BS15 4AW
Tel: Bristol 672977

COARSE FISHING AND FISHERIES

An amalgamation of 11 clubs with waters on the Avon, Chew, Midford Brook, Frome (Bristol) and others

Bristol Avon & District Anglers Consultative Association
J. S. Parker, 16 Lansdown View, Kingswood, Bristol BS15 4AW
Tel: Bristol 672977

Bristol City Docks AC
R. Sims, 65 Sandy Lane, Brislington, Bristol 4

Bristol Golden Carp AA
C. Golding, 24 Queen Street, Two Mile Hill, Kingswood, Bristol BS15 2AZ
Tel: Bristol 677379

Bristol Post Office (Angling Section)
O. W. Edwards, 4 Friezewood Road, Ashton Gate, Bristol
Tel: 665521
Frome (Somerset)

Bristol Reservoirs FFA
C. Ogborne, c/o Glebe Cottage, Rectory Close, Farnborough, Nr Bath

*Bristol Telephones FFA
S. Sparks, 40 Oakdale Court, Downend, Bristol BS16 6DU
Tweed Lake (Coleford)

Bristol and West of England Federation of Anglers
B. Williams, 157 Whiteway Road, Bristol BS5 7RH
Tel: 679226
Avon, Kennet and Avon Canal

British Rail Staff Association (Angling Section)
G. Harcom, 8 Upper Belmont Road, St Andrews, Bristol BS7 9DQ

Calne AA
R. J. Reeves, 16 Wessex Close, Calne, Wilts SN11 8NY
Tel: Calne 814516
Avon, River Marden

Chippenham AC
Mrs M. Steele, 21 Braemor Road, Calne
Tel: 815903
Avon, Peckingell Ponds (Chippenham)

Devizes AC
T. W. Fell, 21 Cornwall Crescent, Devizes, Wilts SN10 5HG
Tel: Trowbridge 5189
Kennet & Avon Canal, Avon (Melksham)

Eden Vale AA
A. A. B. Williams, 57 Lambrook Close, Trowbridge, BA14 9HH
Tel: Trowbridge 765061
Station Road Pond (Westbury)

Flower Pot AA
R. Skuse, 349 Coombs Way, Millers Lodge, North Common, Warmley BS15 5UW
(Refer to Bristol, Bath and Wiltshire Amalgamated Anglers)

Frome and District AA
R. J. Lee, 'Marvic', Keyford Terrace, Frome, Somerset
Tel: Frome 61433
Frome (Somerset), Marston and Berkley Lakes (Frome)

Frome Vale AC
L. Fullbrook, 15a Elmleigh, Mangotsfield, Bristol BS17 3EX
Tel: Bristol 562332
Frome (Bristol)

*Frys AC
Martin Parslow, 32 Aldwick Avenue, Hartcliffe, Bristol
Tel: Bristol 783409
Avon (Keynsham)

Golden Valley FC
S. Hooper, 155a High Street, Bitton
Boyd, Frome (Somerset)

Kelston Anglers
A. Sheppard, 10 Craven Way, The Grange, Warmley, Bristol BS15 5DN
Tel: Bristol 600812
Avon, (Saltford)

Keynsham AA
G. A. Edwards, 10 Clyde Avenue, Keynsham, Bristol
Tel: Bristol 863609
Avon, Chew

Kingswood Disabled AC
G. Thompson, 1 Honey Hill Road, Kingswood, Bristol
Tel: Bristol 671985

King William IV AA
Kevin Boltz, 97 Ferndale Avenue, Longwell Green, Bristol BS15 6XT
Tel: 324619
(Refer to Bristol, Bath and Wiltshire Amalgamated Anglers)

Knowle AC
S. N. Wells, 57 Church Road, Hanham, Bristol

Lavington AC
M. D. Gilbert, Gable Cottage, 24 High Street, Erlestoke, Nr Devizes
Tel: Bratton 425
Semington Brook, Great Cheverell Lake

*Mardon AC
C. J. Austin, 70 Whiteway Road, St George, Bristol
Tel: 558398
Avon (Brislington)

North Somerset & West Wiltshire Federation of Anglers
R. J. Lee, 'Marvic', Keyford Terrace, Frome, Somerset
Tel: Frome 61433
Avon, Boyd

*Purnells FC
M. Hancock, Sunnyside, Tilley Lane, Farmborough, Nr Bath
Tel: Timsbury 70964

Ridgeway AA
R. Walker, 30 Ingleston Road, Wickwar, Wooton-under-edge, Glos GL12 8NH
Tel: Wickwar 749
(Refer to Bristol, Bath and Wiltshire Amalgamated Anglers)

Silver Dace AA
J. Cox, 21 Ingleside Road, Kingswood, Bristol BS15 1HJ

Avon, Frome (Bristol), Frome (Somerset), Chew (refer to Bristol, Bath & Wiltshire Amalgamated Anglers)

Somerfords Fishing Association
D. W. Hitchings, Woodlands, Cleeve Wood Road, Downend, Bristol
Tel: Bristol 568029
Avon, Frome (Bristol), Brinkworth Brook

Stapleton AA
A. Harrison, 18 The Chippings, Southside, Stapleton, Bristol
Tel: Bristol 654799
Avon, Frome (Bristol), River Chew

St George AC
M. Bennett, 20 Talbot Road, Trowbridge, Wilts
Refer to Bristol, Bath & Wiltshire Amalgamated Anglers

Swindon Isis AC
K. D. Sykes, 53 Arnolds Way, Cirencester, Gloucester GL7 1TA
Tel: Cirencester 4994
Avon, Sutton Benger & Kellaways

*SWEB (Angling Section)
D. Hurst, 99 Cock Road, Kingswood, Bristol
Tel: Bristol 606521

*Telephone Manufacturing Co Ltd (ESCC Angling Club)
T. Thomas, 12 Hobbs Close, Malmesbury, Wiltshire
Avon (Malmesbury)

Thatchers AC
R. Miles, c/o Thatchers, 18 Queen Street, Wells
Tel: Wells 73513
Emborough Pond, Midsomer Norton – limited membership

Two Mills FFC
R. Bricknell, 'Tallangatta', The Ley Box, Corsham, Wilts SN14 9IZ
Tel: Box 742749
By Brook, Box

*Ushers AC
M. R. Smart, 11 Kingsdown Road, Trowbridge, Wilts
Tel: Trowbridge 755885

Warminster & District AA
D. M. Vickers, 113 Westleigh, Warminster
Tel: Warminster 215858
Ponds at Shearwater and Dilton, Avon at Pewsham

*Waterside AA (Clark's)
A. Chivers, 57 Specklemead, Paulton, Nr Bristol
Cam Brook

*Westinghouse AC
I. F. Liddell, 76 Brook Drive, Corsham, Wilts

Wootton Bassett AC
T. Strange, 15 Shakespeare Road, Wootton Bassett, Wilts
Brinkworth Brook, Wootton Bassett Lake

NB: *Clubs marked * have membership restrictions*

PRIVATE LAKES

Abbots Pool, Abbots Leigh, Bristol,
Bristol City Council

Bagwood Lake, Patchway, Bristol
Mr Chapman

Blacklands Lakes, Camping & Caravan Park
Mr. J. Walden
Tel: Calne 813672

Bitterwell Lake, Coalpit Heath, Bristol
Mrs Skully, The Chalet, Bitterwell Lake, Coalpit Heath

Brokerswood Lake, Westbury Woodland Park Estate, Brokerswood
Tel: 822238
Limited numbers, book in advance

Erlestoke Lake, Nr Devizes
D. Hampton
Tel: Bratton 830095
Limited day tickets

Ham Green Lake near Pill

Henleaze Lake, Bristol
D. Klemperer, 25 Rockside Drive, Henleaze, Bristol
Tel: Bristol 624748

Ivyhouse Lake, Gittenham
Mr D. Warner, Ivyhouse Farm,
Gittenham, Wilts
Tel: Brinkworth 368

Lakeside, Devizes
Mr Giles, Lakeside Caravan Park,
Caen Hill, Devizes

Longleat Lake
Warminster, Wilts
Tel: Maiden Bradley 551 or Mr Bundy, Tel: Warminster 215082

Leech Pool, Broughton Gifford
Leech Pool Farm, Broughton Gifford, Nr Melksham

Rood Ashton Lake, Trowbridge
Mr Pike, Home Farm, Rood Ashton
Tel: Keevil 870272

Sabre Lake, Calne
Mr P. Candy, Quemerford Gate Farm
Cherhill, Calne
Tel: Calne 812388

Tanhouse Lake, Yate
Tanhouse Farmhouse, Yate Rocks, Yate, Bristol

Witham Friary Lake, Nr Frome
Mr Miles, Witham Hall Farm, Witham Friary
Tel: Nunney 239

FREE FISHING ON THE AVON

Only rod licence required

Bath
Pulteney Weir d/s to Newbridge: along towpath
Bathampton Weir u/s to car park: most of footpath

COARSE FISHING AND FISHERIES

Bristol
Netham Weir u/s to Hanham: towpath only

Chippenham
L.H. bank Radial Gate to Mortimers Wood
R.H. bank Radial Gate to 2 fields d/s

Keynsham
R. Chew confluence: end of recreation ground (L.H. bank), also R. Chew in Keynsham Park

Malmesbury
Sherston Arms u/s of Cascade of Silk Mills
Tetbury Avon u/s Station
Yard Weir – Fire Station (L.H. bank)

DISABLED FACILITIES
Tackenham Lake, near Lyneham
Station Yard, Malmesbury

R/O Council Offices, Monkton Park, Chippenham
R. Marden at Hazeland, Calne
Tucking Mill Lake, Midford, Bath
Sabre Lake, Calne
Kennet & Avon Canal, Devizes
Conham River Park (Kingswood DC)

Avon & Dorset Area

This is dominated by the systems of the Avon on its eastern border with Southern Water plc, the Dorset Stour that shares a joint estuary near Christchurch and the less extensive river Piddle that has a joint estuary with the Dorset Frome in Poole Harbour. And these have important tributaries, especially the Avon which, having wandered down from its beginnings between Devizes and Pewsey in Wiltshire, is joined by no fewer than four streams near Salisbury – Bourne, Wylie, Nadder and Ebble. This is a land of trout and grayling where fishing for the visitor is not readily available.

From Salisbury to the sea the Avon becomes a salmon river of importance, but shares this with a notable range of coarse fish in the specimen class – barbel, roach, dace, chub, grayling, pike among them.

The first fishery reached on the main river is the Services Dry Fly Fishing Association water running the length from Enford to Durrington and made famous by its long-serving 'keeper of the stream' the late Frank Sawyer, as well as the fishing it provides for serving and retired officers of the armed forces. At Amesbury there is a small piece of free fishing, by permission of the local council, then a length to Great Durnford is owned by the Piscatorial Society and, above the city, Salisbury and District AC and this is where the river begins to provide coarse fish as well as trout fishing. The Salisbury District Council issues permits for both trout and coarse fishing at Fisherton. Below the city the local anglingclub has more water until the fishing is taken by London Anglers Association as far as Alderbury, where a long stretch belonging to the Longford & Trafalgar Estate begins, ending at Downton, where fishing can be had from the Bull Hotel and Downton AA. At Fordingbridge various stretches are fished by London Anglers, Salisbury & District and Sandy Balls Estate Ltd and there is a limited piece of free fishing beside the town.

Above the town of Ringwood the river is controlled by Christchurch & District AC after which as far as Christchurch itself you meet the fisheries of Bisterne, Avon Tyrell, Winkton and the renowned Royalty by the town itself. Here one might expect to catch a record chub or barbel at any time!

Of the river's tributaries mentioned, the Bourne is what is known as a winter-bourne and will dry up during the hot summer, but the Wylie is a chalkstream of some note and offers fine sport with trout and grayling. Its lower waters from Steeple Langford hold pike, roach and dace as well and are fished by Wylie FC, Wilton FC and the Salisbury & District club, but there is really only limited opportunity for the visiting coarse fisherman.

The next tributary, the Nadder, is not a true chalk stream, but flows through low-lying meadows and holds (as do so many trout streams of the area) a good stock of dace, perch, roach and pike in its lower reaches, where it is joined at Wilton by the Wylie. Tisbury AC and Teffont FC have lengths further up and Salisbury & District near the city, where the river joins the Avon.

River Stour

Only slightly less regarded than the Avon (and preferred by some coarse fishers), the Stour rises at Stourhead and flows to Gillingham, greatly increasing in capacity as it receives the waters of the Shreen and Lodden. Holding a few trout this river is a coarse fishery from start to finish; these upper reaches have suffered from agricultural pollution severely in the past, but stocks of bream, carp, chub, gudgeon, grayling, perch, roach, dace, tench and pike are hopefully increasing.

At Gillingham the local club's stretch reaches downriver to Stour Provost and the long meandering reach from Marnhull to Sturminster Newton is controlled by Sturminster & Hinton AA, while at Stourpaine Durweston AS has a shorter stretch, after which the Blandford & District has the fishing through Blandford and down to Spettisbury, where Southampton Piscatorials take over as far as Sturminster Marshall, where the Red Spinner AS holds the river to Wimborne Minster. Here Wimborne & District AC have two pieces of water separated by a stretch of free fishing at Canford Bridge, where boats can be hired. Christchurch AC has several stretches along the outer edge of Bournemouth and there is a small free fishery at Redhill, while the well-known Throop fishery has a reputation for big barbel and chub on a par with that of the Royalty.

For the rest of the rivers and streams in this area, both major like Frome and Piddle and minor ones like the Wey, Brit, Bride, Char and Crane (which becomes the Moors river) there is little opportunity for the visiting coarse fisherman except by his own approach to farmers and riparian owners. However, Christchurch AC does have a length above its junction with the Stour.

The area has considerable stillwaters coarse fishing, much of it of very high calibre, but this also is jealousy preserved for club members only in many cases. However, the list of fisheries on page 78 providing either mixed game and coarse or coarse fishing alone may be of use, while enquiries to listed angling clubs can also elicit the most up-to-date information about waters under their control ... and, of course, we get back to the basic sources – licence distributors and tackle dealers.

STILLWATERS

Perhaps we should follow the courses of the rivers already considered, adjacent to which lie most of the stillwater fisheries.

The Avon valley offers little but Peter's Finger Lakes just south of Salisbury, where small lakes have been formed among old gravel workings and are well-stocked with carp, tench and bream.

Close to the Wylie on the Longleat estate, Shearwater Lake is a fairly large water affording good fishing for tench and bream and permits should be obtained from the estate office at Longleat House. At Steeple Langford gravel extraction has created some lakes and these hold bream, carp, roach and tench and are controlled by Salisbury & District AC.

Near the river Nadder are several well-stocked pools, but all are restricted. At the top of the river Stour, however, day permits for coarse fishing are available for Turner's Paddock – a small lake owned by the National Trust – and these should be obtained from a kiosk at the entrance to the gardens at Stourhead. A little further south Gasper Lakes also provide one water for fishing by permit and near Broadstone Creekmoor Pond is an excellent coarse fishery run by Wimborne & District AC and Poole Borough Council, where permits can be had from the Town Clerk's office. The club also has fishing at Kingsbridge Lakes, Lytchett Minster and the council offers free fishing at Blue Pool, Hamworthy.

South of Dorchester on the river Frome you find Warmell Ponds and Pallington Lakes. The first are several small gravel pits stocked with coarse fish and available to the visiting angler, who will also be welcomed at Pallington, where a pool is stocked with coarse fish, another with trout. In Dorchester, John Aplin's tackle shop can sell permits to fish Luckfield Lake near Broadmayne while Wally's Lakes near Osmington Mills can be fished on ticket from the Ranch House. In the Wareham area a number of small lakes provide coarse fishing and Creech Lake is fished exclusively by the Wareham & District AC. Wessex NRA holds fishing rights on the tidal parts of Frome and Piddle and allows anglers to fish the former free below South Bridge providing they possess a licence.

As its name suggests the river Wey empties into the sea at Weymouth after running through Radipole Lake – a large and interesting piece of water holding carp, eels, dace and roach as well as bream and tench. Although controlled by the Civil Service Angling Society, permits can be had from tackle shops in the town and from the local council offices. A certain head of coarse fish has moved upstream into the river and permission to fish can sometimes be obtained from local farmers.

ANGLING CLUB SECRETARIES

Blandford & District AC
Mrs J. Leslie, 20 Fields Oak,
Blandford Forum, Dorset
DT11 7PP

Christchurch AC
K. Hall, 32 Wycliffe Road,
Bournemouth BH9 1JS
Tel: Bournemouth 518540

Devizes AA
T. W. Fell, 21 Cornwall
Crescent, Devizes
SN10 5HG
Tel: Devizes 5189

Dorchester & District AS
J. Parkes, 5 Malta Close,
Dorchester, Dorset, DT1 1QT

Dorchester FC
J. J. Fisher, 'Rew Hollow',
Godmanstone, Dorchester,
Dorset DT2 7AH
Tel: Cerne Abbas 306

Downton AA
B. Hayward, 37 Bridge
Street, Fordingbridge, Hants
Tel: Fordingbridge 56330

Durweston AS
J. H. Thatchell, Methody,
Durweston, Nr Blandford,
Dorset

Gillingham & District AA Ltd
J. R. K. Stone, Ferndale,
Ham, Gillingham, Dorset
SP8 4LL
Tel: Gillingham 2386

London AA
Mrs P. Ellis, Forest Road Hall, Hervey Park Road,
London E17 6LJ
Tel: 01 520 7477

Longleat Estate
River Wylye Fishing
R. B. Charles, The Estate Office, Longleat,
Warminster, Wilts
Tel: Maiden Bradley 324

Marlborough & District AA
M. Ellis, 'Failte', Elcot Close,
Marlborough, Wilts
Tel: Marlborough 52922

Pewsey & District AA
Mrs M Draper, 'Mardale', 14 Haines Terrace, Pewsey,
Wilts SN9 5DX

The Piscatorial Society
J. H. S. Hunt, Starlings, 76 High Street, Market Lavington, Devizes, Wilts
Tel: Lavington 3357

Ringwood & District A of A
R. C. Smith, 1 Avon Castle Drive, Ringwood, Hants
Tel: Ringwood 472642

Salisbury & District AC
R. W. Hillier, 29 New Zealand Avenue, Salisbury,
Wilts, SP2 7JZ
Tel: Salisbury 21164

Services Dry FFA
Col D. A. N. C. Miers, H.Q.,

Salisbury Plain Training Area, Bulford, Salisbury,
Wilts SP4 9PA
Tel: (0980) 33371 x 2382 (Office)

Southampton Piscatorial Society
P. J. Dowse, 33 Arnheim Road, Lordswood,
Southampton, Hants
Tel: Southampton 766512

Sturminster & Hinton AA
T. J. Caines, Coombe Gate,
The Bridge, Sturminster Newton, Dorset
Tel: Sturminster Newton 72355

Warminster & District AC
D. M. M. Vickers, 113 Westleigh, Warminster, Wilts
BA12 8NJ
Tel: Warminster 215858

Wilton Fly FC
E. J. Hunt, Lee Mill Cottage,
Leegomery, Telford TF1 4QD
Tel: Telford 52374

Wimborne & District AC
Steve Piper, 131 Verity Crescent, Canford Heath,
Poole, Dorset BH17 7TU
Tel: Poole 683008

OTHER FISHERIES

Knights in the Bottom Fishery
Hooke, Beaminster, Dorset

Langford Fishery
Steeple Langford, Salisbury,
Wilts

Mangerton Lake
Mangerton, Bridport, Dorset

Myrtle Farm Fishery
Waytown, Bridport, Dorset

Pallington Lakes
Mr Clarke, Tincleton,
Dorchester, Dorset
Tel: Puddletown 8141

Philinda Ltd
P. Cook, Whitesheet Trout Lakes, Whitesheet,
Wimborne, Dorset
Tel: Wimborne 842772

Rawlsbury Waters
High Ansty, Dorset
Tel: (0258) 880349

Rockbourne Trout Fisheries Ltd
Tony Hern, Rockbourne Road, Sandleheath,
Fordingbridge, Hants SP6 1QG
Tel: Rockbourne 603

Wessex Fly Fishing School
R. Slocock, Lawrences Farm,
Tolpuddle, Dorchester,
Dorset DT2 7HF
Tel: Puddletown 8460

Zeals Fish Farms
5 Canham, Green Stones,
Wolverton, Zeals,
Warminster, Wilts
Tel: Bourton 840573

OTHER USEFUL ADDRESSES

Royalty Fishery
The Fisheries Officer, West Hants Water Company,
Knapp Mill, Mill Road,
Christchurch, Dorset BH23 2JH
Tel: Christchurch 485262

Throop Fisheries
The School House,
Holdenhurst Village,
Bournemouth, Dorset
Tel: Bournemouth 515469

Somerset Area

This is a maze of waterways where streams flow down from the hills to a great plain, where rivers run parallel with their accompanying drains towards the Bristol Channel with a network of inter-connecting ditches, dykes or rhynes draining the wide wetlands, as the Somerset Levels are also known. For the game fisherman opportunity is very limited except on the well-stocked stillwaters splendidly managed by Bristol Waterworks Company Ltd and Wessex Water plc. But here the coarse fisherman can enjoy a wide variety as well as widespread opportunities to fish meandering waterways, large and small. And there is good fishing to be had, too, in numerous lakes and clay pits in the area.

The area contains six catchments and the many miles of banks each contain are fished by numerous angling associations; for simplicity I shall describe each system briefly and list those clubs with fisheries along its length and shall then list the stillwaters available to anglers, excluding many very small ponds holding fish, but often over-fished.

First, however, a brief survey of the area and its main towns where tackle shops are available. The western boundary is the Bristol Channel running south from Portishead to Burnham-on-Sea where the coast turns sharply westward to Minehead and Exmoor. The southern boundary turns back along the hills to enclose Wellington, Ilminster and Yeovil. The eastern border then runs northwards around Sherborne, Shepton Mallet, Cheddar, and Bristol Waterwork's Blagdon Lake. In the heart of the area are the towns of Taunton, Langport, Ilchester, Street, Glastonbury, Bridgwater, Highbridge and back along the coast north of Burnham, Weston-super-Mare and Clevedon.

Tone Catchment
The source of this river is in the far west of the area where a stream springs from Brendon Hill, feeds the trout fishery at Clatworthy reservoir and flows on through steep wooded valleys to Taunton. Both the Tone and its several tributaries, of which the Hillfarrance Brook is the major, are ideal trout waters and as such are strictly preserved. However, as the river nears Taunton, increasing in size and depth, grayling, chub, dace and roach begin to appear and at the town between French Weir and Firepool Weir fishing is free for those with an NRA licence. At Firepool the Bridgwater & Taunton Canal joins the river and below the weir the water runs fast, but at Bathpool the Tone changes to deeper, slower water and roach, bream, tench, carp and pike become the usual species found. Along this stretch where the river runs through moor and marsh much of the fishing is controlled by Taunton AA, while the river above Taunton is in the hands of the Taunton Fly Fishing Club and Wellington AA. From New Bridge the water can be affected by high tides and at Stanmoor Bridge it joins forces with the river Parrett.

West Sedgemoor Main Drain
Parallel with the lower reaches of the Tone runs this artificial channel built in the '40s along the lines of old water courses draining the West Sedge Moor. It is popular as a match venue and holds carp and tench, but is especially good for bream and roach. Here the fishing is again available through Taunton AA.

Bridgwater & Taunton Canal

Created in 1827 this canal runs from Taunton to join the river Parrett at Bridgwater Dock. Although containing little deep water the canal does offer excellent fishing for all the coarse fish of the area, including pike and perch as well as rudd, and specimen fish are by no means uncommon. Access is again simple enough as the canal is more or less divided between Taunton AA and Bridgwater AA.

Parrett & Isle Catchment

The river Parrett has a long run from Crewkerne in West Dorset joining forces with the river Isle (which rises near Chard) above Langport and with the river Yeo below that town. Its headwaters are reserved for trout, but there is coarse fishing on the Isle and at Langport the Parrett becomes a coarse fishery of importance, noted for fine catches of bream. All the other coarse fish of the area are caught as well and the river grows as it takes on water of the Isle. Now wide and deep the river remains fishable throughout its length to the point where the levels are controlled by Oath sluice, after which it is tidal. But running almost parallel and to the east to join the Parrett below Bridgwater is the King's Sedgemoor Drain, constructed in the late eighteenth century and a fishery in its own right.

Fishing rights along the Parrett are held by Stoke-sub-Hamdon AA, Wessex Federation and Langport AA. On the Isle clubs concerned are Chard AA, Ilminster AA, and Newton Abbot AA.

The King's Sedgemoor Drain is a continuation of the river Cary and considered a watershed of its own with two minor subsidiaries draining the moors to east and west. All fishing is controlled by Bridgwater AA.

Yeo Catchment

The river Yeo joins the Parrett below Langport and stems from Seven Sisters' Well, joining the stream from Sherborne Lake, after which it is augmented by the river Wriggle and Sutton Bingham stream flowing from that trout reservoir. The tributaries are entirely trout preserves, but the main river has a mixed fishery between Sherborne and Yeovil. Below this town a series of weirs provide deeper water and conditions are ideal for the coarse fish. The Yeo moves on through open country to Ilchester and runs on through King's Moor and Wet Moor before linking with the larger river.

Fishing rights are held by Yeovil & Sherborne AA (including a length of the river Wriggle) and by Ilchester & District AA.

Brue Catchment

The river Brue rises east of Bruton and is a preserved trout fishery as far as Lydford. Here, where it passes under the A37 a section of river is fished by Bristol & District Amalgamated Anglers, after which Glaston Manor AA have rights over a length of weirs and deeper water providing some notable chub fishing as far as Butt Moor, after which the Brue is banked and runs through the wide plain dominated by Glastonbury Tor and is joined by a number of drains, also by the river Sheppey on which Glaston Manor AA also have the fishing. Roach, bream, dace and pike now feature among the species of fish and are to be found all the final length of the course to Highbridge, channelled through the Somerset Levels and connected with large excavated waterways like the Huntspill River and South Drain by way of the Cripps River. The Huntspill is one of the best known venues for important national match competitions, when bags generally consist of roach and bream.

Fishing rights on this catchment are held by the following clubs: Glaston Manor AS, Bristol Amalgamated Anglers, Bridgwater AA, North Somerset AA.

Axe Catchment
The river Axe emerges from the Mendip Hills as a trout water until its depth increases when it reaches the flat lowlands at the foot of the hills where dace, roach, chub and pike become the main fish for the angler until the river becomes channelled and bream and tench join the list to the sluices at Bleadon and Brean Cross, after which the Axe is tidal. Among its tributaries are a number of rhynes and the Cheddar Yeo and Lox Yeo, both of which hold good stocks of coarse fish.

The Hixham Rhyne is another man-made drain in the catchment and holds bream and roach. And to the north of the area three other courses reach the sea near Clevedon – the Congresbury Yeo, river Kenn and the New Blind Yeo, a drainage channel dug to carry excess waters from the river. The first river rises in the Mendips and flows into and out of Blagdon Lake, where it is preserved as a trout fishery, to Wrington where it can be fished for dace, roach and rudd. Kenn and Blind Yeo offer a wider selection of coarse fish, including perch, pike, tench and bream and fishing on all is controlled by Bristol & District Amalgamated anglers and the North Somerset Association of ACs.

Fishing rights in the Axe system are held by Bristol Amalgamated Anglers, North Somerset Association, Cheddar AC and Bristol & District AA, details may be obtained from tacklists in the area and association secretaries (see list).

ANGLING ASSOCIATIONS

Bridgwater AA
I. Williams, 2 Webbers Way, Puriton, Bridgwater
Huntspill River, Cripps River, South Drain, North Drain, Kings Sedgemoor Drain, 18 Foot Rhyne, Langacre Rhyne, Bridgwater/Taunton Canal, Dunwear Ponds, Screech Owl Ponds, Combwich Ponds, Walrow Ponds, Highbridge.

Bristol, Bath & Wilts Amalgamated Anglers
J. S. Parker, 16 Lansdown View, Kingswood, Bristol BS15 4AW
River Axe, River Brue, River Yeo (Congresbury): Brickyard Ponds, Pawlett; Other waters outside the Somerset Area.

Chard AA
M. Lillywhite, 38 Wellings Close, South Chard, Somerset TA20 2RY

River Isle (also Perry St Pond, South Chard and River Otter in NRA South West Region)

Cheddar AC
A. T. Lane, 1 Orchard Close, Cheddar, Somerset
River Axe, Hixham Rhyne, Cheddar Claypits, Cheddar Reservoir, North Drain

Clevedon & District Freshwater AC
D. A. Harper, 5 Kingsley Road, Clevedon, Avon
Further details: See North Somerset Association of Angling Clubs

Glaston Manor AA
J. Ogden, 10 Dovecote Close, Farm Lane, Street Somerset
River Brue, South Drain and all other waters within the Glaston XII Hides.

Highbridge AA
J. Underhill, 215 Berrow Rd, Burnham-on-Sea, Somerset
Further details: See North Somerset Association of Angling Clubs

Ilchester and District AA
B. Bushell, 1 Friars Close, Ilchester, Somerset.
River Yeo

Ilminster and District AA
P. Lonton, Mashala, Cottage Corner, Ilton, Ilminster, Somerset.
River Isle

Langport and District AA
J. B. Phillips, 4 Brooklands Rd, Huish Episcopi, Langport
River Parrett

Newton Abbot AA
D. Horder, 22 Mount Pleasant Road, Newton Abbot, Devon
River Isle

North Somerset Association of Angling Clubs (Member Clubs Clevedon, Highbridge and Weston-super-Mare)
R. Newton, 64 Clevedon Road, Tickenham, Clevedon, Avon BS21 6RD
Rivers Keen, New Blind Yeo, Axe, Brue, North Drain, South Drain, Congresbury Yeo, Cheddar Yeo, Newtown Lake, Apex Ponds and Walrow Ponds, Highbridge; Locking Pit, Weston-super-Mare, together with some smaller rivers.

Stoke-sub-Hamdon and District AA
D. Goad, 2 Windsor Lane, Stoke-sub-Hamdon, Somerset.
River Parrett

Taunton AA
H. King, 145 Henson Park, Chard, Somerset
River Tone, Bridgwater/Taunton Canal, West Sedgemoor Main Drain, Ponds at Norton Fitzwarren, Wych Lodge Lake

Taunton Fly Fishing Club
J. Hill, 21 Manor Road, Taunton, Somerset
River Tone (plus short stretches on River Axe in NRA South West Region)

Wessex Federation of Angling Clubs
J. J. Mathrick, Perham Farmhouse, Wick, Langport, Somerset TA10 0NN
Rivers Parrett and Isle.

Weston-super-Mare and District AA
K. Tucker, 26 Coniston Crescent, Weston-super-Mare, Avon
Further details: See North Somerset Association of Angling Clubs.

Wellington AA
M. Cave, 1 Chitterwell Cottage, Sampford Arundell, Wellington, Somerset
River Tone

Windmill AA
N. Gooding, 11 Chilkwell Street, Glastonbury, Somerset, BA6 8DL
Butleigh Lake

Yeovil and Sherborne AA
N. Garrett, 18 Springfield Road, Yeovil, Somerset
Rivers Yeo and Wriggle, Sutton Bingham Stream, Sherborne Lake

Some waters listed are only available to adult season ticket holders of the clubs concerned.

STILLWATERS FISHERIES (*Over two acres*)

Apex Pond
Highbridge, Somerset (North Somerset AA)

Bristol Bridge Ponds
Highbridge, Somerset

The Beeches Carp Ponds
Westonzoyland Road,
Bridgwater, Somerset

Chard Reservoir
Chard, Somerset

Cheddar Reservoir
Cheddar, Somerset (Cheddar AA)

Combwich Ponds
Combwich, Bridgwater
(Bridgwater AA)

Dunwear Ponds
Dunwear, Bridgwater
(Bridgwater AA)

Newtown Pond
Highbridge (North Somerset AA)

Screech Owl Pond
Huntworth, Bridgwater
(Bridgwater AA)

The Sedges
Dunwear Lane, Dunwear,
Bridgwater

Sherborne Lake
Sherborne, Dorset (Yeovil & Sherborne AA)

Walrow Ponds
Highbridge (Bridgwater & North Somerset AA)

The South West Region

I have already explained that coarse fisheries are by no means natural to the rivers of Devon and Cornwall, but rudd in particular seem to have been indigenous to the many small pools, often flooded quarries and pits sometimes hidden away in the privacy of deep woodland, for many years: I have also found very large perch in some. Also the few man-made waterways like the canals at Bude, Tiverton and Exeter as well as the lower, deeper reaches of some rivers hold roach, rudd, tench, carp, perch, pike and bream according to the suitability of the water.

Where small stillwater fisheries have been developed carp and tench generally predominate and produce some very fine specimens.

Permits for most of these waters can be had from tacklists and it is best to name these in connection with the name of the nearest town, also to give telephone numbers where these exist.

Do not forget that within the region of the NRA SW there is no close season for coarse fish and anglers are often able to fish throughout the year.

DEVON

Barnstaple Venn Pond. Permits from town's tackle shop. River Taw: membership (full and temporary) Barnstaple & District AA from A. J. Penny, Endswell House, Raleigh Road, Barnstaple.

Berrynarbor Mill Pond, one acre at Mill Park Touring Caravan and Camping, Berrynarbor, Combe Martin. Tel: Combe Martin 2647.

Bideford Jennets (see South West Water)

Bovey Tracey Blue Water (see Exeter). Bradley Ponds (see Newton Abbot AA). Trenchford Reservoir: pike (see SWW)

Braunton One acre lake at Little Comfort Farm. Tel: Braunton 812414

Chard Perry Street Pond. Contact Chard Angling Centre, 89a Fore Street; Chard Cycle Co., Holyrood St or Rose Cottage adjacent to pond.

Clovelly Five acre lake at Clovelly Country Club, East Yagland, Woolsery, nr Bideford. Tel: Clovelly 442 04 448

Cullompton Two acre lake. Tel: Bickleigh 248

Dartmouth Old Mill reservoir (see SWW)

Exeter Squabmoor (see SWW). Hogsbrook Lake 2½ acres at Greendale Barton Farm, Woodbury Salterton. Tel: Exeter 68183.

Upham Farm carp ponds at Farringdon. Tel: Woodbury 32247

Exeter & District AA has considerable waters on river Exe, Culm and Creedy as well as on the six miles of Exeter Canal and sundry stillwaters. Permits, membership and maps can be had from tackle shops in Exeter – Angling Centre, Smythen Street; Tony Gould, Longbrook Street; Gun & Sports, Heavitree; Bridge Cafe at Countess Wear; Topsham Ferry; PK Angling, Clifton Road and the Tourist Information Centre. Also at tacklists in Crediton, Cullompton, Exmouth, Newton Abbot, Tiverton and Torquay.

Halwill Anglers Paradise Holidays has eight fishing lakes near Beaworthy. Tel: Beaworthy 559.

Honiton Hollies Trout Farm has a small pond at Sheldon. Tel: Broadhembury 428.

Ilfracombe Slade reservoir (see SWW).

Kenton Home Farm Pond, one acre (see Exeter & District AA).

Kingsbridge Coombe Fishery, one acre, contact Kingsbridge 2038.

Kingsteignton Abbrook Pond (see Exeter & District AA). Preston Ponds, four lakes (see Newton Abbot FA).

Newton Abbot Decoy Lake one and a half acre. Contact Teignbridge District Council Countryside Ranger. Tel: Newton Abbot 61101 ex 2742.
Rackerhayes Ponds: five lakes controlled by Newton Abbot AA who accept associate membership and allow a permit holder to bring junior anglers under 10 to fish free of charge. Permits are obtainable from Drum Sports and the Angling Centre in NA; The Anglers Den, Brixham; Paignton Sports in Paignton; Plainmoor Angling Centre, Torquay; Blake Sports at Totnes and the Angling Centre in Exeter.
Trago Mills has 600 yards of fishing from March 1 to November 30 and contact should be made with the warden on NA 462.

Okehampton South Reed Fisheries: $3^{1}/_{2}$ acre lake on nature reserve. Barbless hooks only available on site where tackle can be hired. Tel: Bratton Clovelly 295

Swimbridge Riverton Fishery near Barnstaple: two lakes 3 & 4 acres. Tackle and barbless hooks available on site. Tel: Barnstaple 830009.

Tiverton Grand Western Canal (closed March 15–June 15): contact Canal Liaison Officer on Craddock 40807 or local tackle shops for permits. Sampford Peverell Ponds (contact Exeter AA)

Torrington Darracott reservoir (see SWW).

CORNWALL

Bodmin Lake View Country Club at Lanivet 831808. Three good pools

Bude Lower Tamar Lake (see SWW). One and quarter miles canal (closed April–May): contact Bude AA

Falmouth College reservoir (see SWW)

Helston/Penzance area Marazion AC controls fishing on a number of 2 acre ponds, Boscathnoe reservoir $3^{1}/_{2}$ acres and Wheal Grey Pool – a 4-acre lake. Day and week permits: contact The Shop at Newtown or phone for membership on Penzance 65638

Launceston Alder Quarry $4^{1}/_{2}$ acres. Details Tel: Lewdown 444
Dutson Water Tel: Launceston 2607 or 6456
Stone Lake, $4^{1}/_{2}$ acres Tel: Bridestowe 253
Tredidon Barton Lake, only $^{3}/_{4}$ acre Tel: Pipers Pool 86 288

Liskeard A small pond at Badham Farm, St Keyne Tel: Liskeard 43572

Newquay Porth reservoir (see SWW)

Penzance see Helston. Also two lakes available at St Buryan Tel: 810220. Tindeen Fishery, Three pools Tel: Germoe 3486

Perranporth Four acre lake. Permits on site one mile from Perranporth. Contact Truro 572388

St Mawes Trenestrall Lake, 2 acres. Details Tel: Truro 501259

Saltash Crafthole reservoir 3 acres (see SWW).
Two acre lake at St Germans. Royal Albert Bridge AC. Permits from Brokenshires, Saltash Road, Keyham, Plymouth, The Tackle Box, Exeter Street, Bill's Tackle Box, Albert Road in Plymouth and Godfrey's in Station Road, Liskeard.

Truro Mellonwatts Mill Fishery: $2^{1}/_{4}$ acre pond on main road from Grampound to Mevagissey. Details Tel: Tregony 232 Langarth Pool, only $^{3}/_{4}$ acre at Threemilestone. Contact Truro 75638

NOTE Local tackle shops will be able to give directions for access to these fisheries, but I suggest that a telephone call will enable the angler to obtain the latest information as well as directions to each location and news of fishing. It is also worth considering that many fisheries can provide accommodation or recommend it.

7
BAIT FISHING FOR SEA TROUT

As a readily available bait, freely accepted by a wide variety of fish, the humble earthworm has probably caught more budding anglers their first fish – be it gudgeon, daddy-ruffe, perch or chub *et al* – and where the wild brown trout swims free in the streams and rivers to which it is indigenous it is a redworm, brandling or lob which catches most fish for young fishermen and, indeed, goes on providing sport for a great many rods throughout their lives.

The worm can be used in more diverse ways than any other bait, natural or artificial: it can also be fished in places beloved by the more secretive of fishes where natural obstacles make the casting of a fly, even the working of a spoon ineffective at the best and impossible at worst. Maggot and wasp grubs are also extremely killing, but as they may be employed in the same way as worms I include their use in this chapter.

There is one way of using a maggot which really comes under the fly fishing heading. It is to garnish one's fly with one, as is commonly practised by anglers fishing for sewin by night on Welsh rivers ... as I used one on the point of my fly when fishing for chub with a big, bushy fly under Thameside willows in the days when the blow fly's progeny were called gentles!

West Country peal also love maggots, but until very recently it was a bait little known and virtually unobtainable (unless you bred them at home) until opportunities for coarse fishing developed and with the coarse fishermen there came the demand for their favourite bait.

But here a word of caution is timely. The use of natural baits may well be restricted to certain stretches of some rivers by bye-laws covering the fishery. It is banned altogether on some in Devon, while no such restrictions are applied to Cornish waters. But beware of bye-laws ... they must be obeyed, of course, but if they imply that you may feel free to fish by any acceptable means you choose it is very possible that the owner of a part of a river or the angling club whose water you are fishing apply their own limits to fishing methods, baits to be used, number of fish which may be retained – even size limits greater than those applied by the higher authority. Such need not be block bans, but apply only to certain parts of the fishing covered by your permit!

There is no time, nor are there any acceptable conditions of weather or water when the fish – brownie, sea trout or salmon – *may not* take a natural bait properly presented. There are times, however, when any of these quarry *will not* take the offering. This is more often than not the fault of the fisherman – not necessarily he who presents the bait, but those who have passed that way before him. In its

19 An angler being rescued from a watery grave in the river Camel.

20 A licensed netsman on the Teign shows Derek Clifton, NRA Fisheries Inspector for South Devon, the fruits of five hours' labour. (*Photo: NRA*)

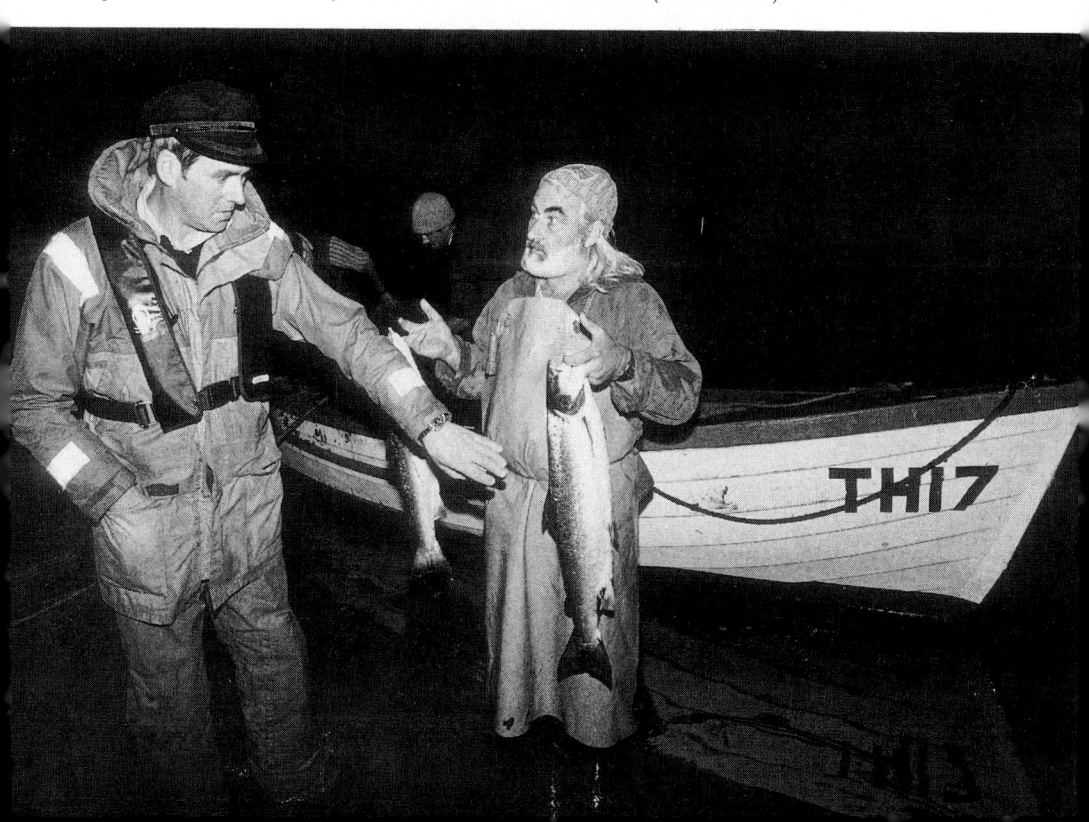

21 Sampling Officer Antoinette Headon collecting water samples at Burrator Reservoir. (*Photo: John Lyne*)

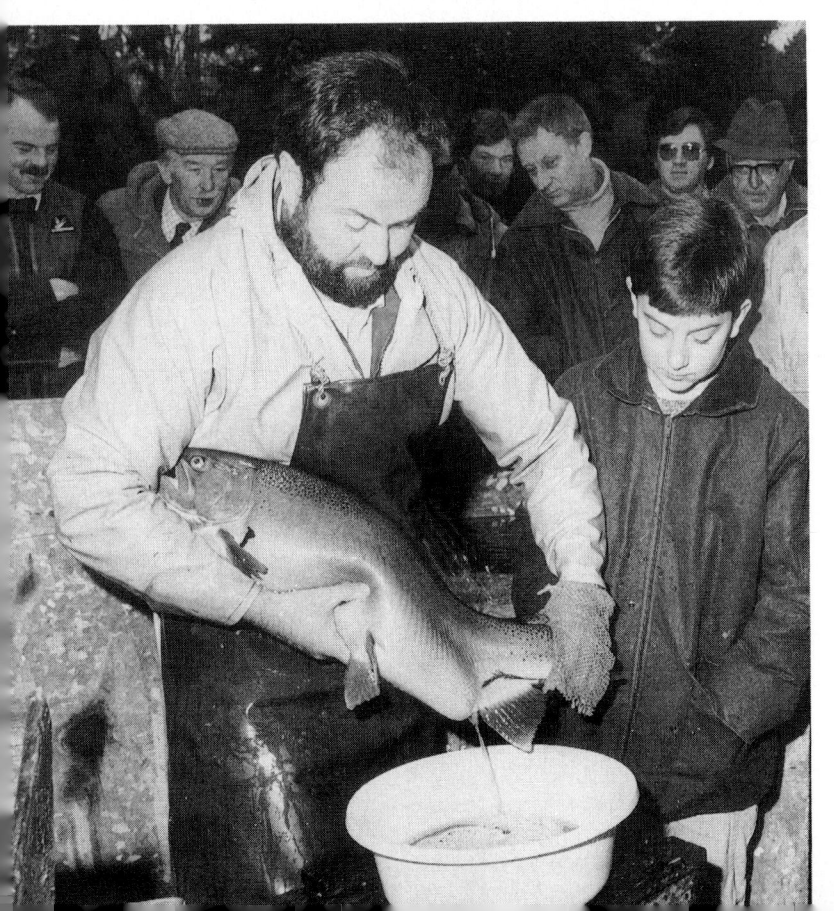

22 Bristol Waterworks hatchery man at Ubley, Andrew Mayo, spawning a prime brood fish, watched by members of the Bristol Reservoirs Fly Fishers' Association. (*Photo: Bristol Waterworks Company*)

course upriver from the sea the migratory fish must run a gauntlet of shining bits of metal, each twisting, spinning, rising and diving across its path or over its resting place: concoctions of feather and tinsel, some brightly hued, some sombre passing across the current as well as big prawns boiled red and little shrimps of natural dress or multi-coloured and the aforementioned grubs and worms. Familiarity breeds contempt and if the fish has not already fallen for some part of this multiplicity of deceits there comes a time – usually when the river has been low and clear for some days, but also when all other conditions seem perfect – salmon and sea trout say, 'Enough!'

The stay-at-home brown trout, territorially minded as it is, is a captive audience of the show put on for its bigger brethren, which is why few brownies live long enough to grow big in the lower reaches of West Country rivers and the best of the sport with these delightful fish is to be had way up the rivers and in the smaller tributaries and feeders, where later the migrants will arrive on big water to select the gravels for spawning.

To a greater or lesser degree all methods of fishing for sea trout and salmon are enhanced when there is some colour in the water: both *salar* and *trutta* will stir from their lethargy at the first signs of a coming spate – as the river begins to rise and through the first four or five inches, for half-an-hour or so to an hour, until the river begins to come down dirty, not just stained. During that brief period the fly will work, the spoon will take fish, after which the carefully presented bait may tempt both salmon and sea trout when fished close in under the bank, in eddies off the main current and where rocks and boulders or conformations in the bed of the river provide lies sheltered from the main force of the flood.

This sudden activity by the fish may be due to the immediate instinct that a freshet is on its way, which, in turn, rekindles the urge to continue the journey upstream. If the rise in water is sufficient and sustained both species will start to run – a time when the salmon is never tempted to turn aside to attack a spoon bait, even if it could see it, or take time off to use its olfactory sense to seek out a bunch of lobworms. The sea trout behaves in a similar manner, but does on occasion give the rod some sport when running. This is probably because brief runs inspired by the sudden rains of high summer are of short duration: sometimes a shoal of peal will leave a pool as the river rises, reach another only a short way further upstream, linger there only to drop back to their starting point as the river runs off and the water clears. Under other conditions when high water is sustained over a period of days or the river's force is very fierce or the water dirty with solids in suspension, sea trout may progress in a series of spurts, resting awhile in between. When this happens the fish become rather spread out as each seeks its own temporary respite from the current before making another move upriver.

At such times a spinner can be lethal when used to search all those places which offer shelter, even where the water is relatively shallow – a fast run rather than a pool. Bait can also be used at this time, but is probably best suited for use searching the slacks and eddies close to the bank and especially where boulders, promontaries or tree roots and fallen trunks may act as stops against the stream. In fact, when the river is really dirty the water close to the bank offers the only hope for a fish to find a home and for your worms to find the fish.

From the time the flood turns and the water clears, progressively both spoon and worm become increasingly effective; but on spate rivers today this can be a very brief period indeed – the top of the sport available only for a few hours or a day or two at best. Rivers rising away from the moors and pursuing their courses through alluvial plains take longer to run off and offer a more prolonged period when conditions for fishing – be it with fly, spinner or bait – remain in the anglers' favour.

As a river becomes smaller in size and its water clearer and clearer, so the use of spinner and the daytime use of fly become fruitless – with some exceptions – where peal are concerned, but the ubiquitous worm will still catch fish.

Many, many years ago I found a great fat trout lying in a little pool behind the weeds of a famous Cotswolds trout stream. The water of that limestone river is as clear as crystal and the fish lay in comparatively shallow water below the main flow of the current over the weed beds. It would not take a fly, so I offered it a worm, fished in the best upstream tradition .. except that each time I dropped the bait into the water just below the tail of the weeds so that it would drift gently down past the fish's nose, the trout took fright and bolted downstream and across river to the security of its holt under the bank.

However, the fish betrayed its own sense of security by returning to the same pool after a few minutes. So, I moved up to a position on the bank level with the tail of the weeds and, on my belly, swung the hooked worm in a casual arc to land a foot upstream of the fish: this time, however, I had 'bitten on' a couple of split shot – sufficient to hold the bait to the bottom – on the 4X cast about a foot above the hook. The heavy fly line remained above the surface and the light cast caused no drag from the stream. My trout (which had, of course, bolted again) duly returned and lay poised in the gentle current, apparently oblivious of the two luscious worms wriggling on the size 10 hook – an old fly I had stripped for the purpose.

But that fish knew the bait was there and, after a minute which seemed an hour, dropped back on the current and with a quick twist of its body fell on the worms with very much the same lust as a terrier twists on a rat ... and the prize was mine – not so much the fish as the lesson learned.

Because much of what applies to *salmo fario* also applies to *salmo trutta*, we can redeem an otherwise fishless day by resorting to what I have always referred to as the 'tethered goat' principle – substituting worm for goat, of course – once we have located a likely shoal of sea trout. Keep out of sight, cast your weighted worm, see the shoal disperse, wait, silent and invisible, until the schoolies reassemble. You can take two or three peal before the game is up!

The art of this little deception lies in the end tackle used. You are dealing with a powerful fish, even if the school holds nothing heavier than $1^{1}/_{2}$ lb; but you are also competing against a very shy and sensitive one whose senses for survival – sight and sound – are multiplied by powers of communication with the shoal ... the one being physical and demonstrable, the other which can only be described by what we know as telepathy. If you find a big school of peal lying in line astern, as they like to do under the bank or the shade of overhanging trees or lying over the expanse of a pool, sun-dappled by the tree foliage above, you have only to disturb the least of them all – the little fellow lying unnoticed at the very end of the shoal. He bolts and they all bolt, but the shoal reassembles in due course of time. It is similar to the occasion when casting a fly to a shoal of grayling the fall or flash of the line upsets one fish and in a couple of seconds the entire population is – as dear old Frank Sawyer used to describe it, 'milling around all over the place'. Those fish will settle again, given time, but remain sullen and suspicious much longer than the panic lasted. The worst situation which in turn becomes a hopeless one is when a good school is lying deep in the water and becomes aware of the fact that all is not well. You are not to know why or how they sensed danger; all you will know is that where at one moment there were grey shadows of fish there is nothing! What was there is gone, evaporated, dispersed . . . and you did not see the going of it.

I have stressed the need for the angler to remain unseen and unheard by his quarry: at the same time daylight fishing in clear water demands that he take risks in balancing his tackle against the conditions and the power of the quarry. Whether you are fishing upstream with worm, a tiny Devon or a nymph you will have to take risks: use a leader of a breaking strain which may seem to be on the verge of suicidal!

I am positively averse to using tackle too light for the task it is required to do: not only is it pointless to hook a fish only to lose it, but it is very unfair. On the other hand it is possible to reduce the odds on a breakage by using carefully balanced tackle and considerable personal constraint.

This gamble is not on if the water you intend to fish contains more than a reasonable amount of hazard: the intention to hook and land your fish remains. To hook it, to get it to take whatever offering you have in mind automatically means the use of fine monofilament – probably not more than 2 lb BS against the 6 lb you will employ at night! In turn, this demands a gentle tightening into the fish when it takes and nothing remotely like 'a strike', which is an action I have studiously avoided in all forms of river fishing since an early age. Once the sea trout is on you will need 'hands' to play it successfully and the long, soft full-length actioned rod, which is the exact opposite of my favourite dry fly outfit.

Whether fly fishing or long-trotting a bait you need a light leader, a light line and a rod which will lift the latter off the water quickly. The best I ever met for this purpose was a greenheart fly rod which I used to cast a very light float tackle baited with hempseed into swims under the far bank of Shakespeare's Avon. To take those roach one needed a sharpness of eye combined with an immediate response from the wrist and a rod that obeyed orders without delay. Unfortunately, by the time I met my first peal the greenheart was but a memory!

The rods you quite definitely should not bring into your quest for *trutta* when bait fishing with light tackle is a sharp-actioned one of carbon fibre, no matter how expensive, or a short stiff spinning rod of any material, excellent though it may be for its specific purpose. A spinning rod is for spinning or, maybe, ledgering a worm for salmon in deep and heavy water.

The length of the rod is also a source of misunderstanding: many anglers believe that relatively small rivers and streams with their attendant overhanging herbage and tunnels of branches so beloved by sea trout demand the use of short rods. Many angling writers refer to the fun to be had when using a $7^1/_2$-ft cane, carbon or glass rod and a light line for the 'little breakfast trout' as Dermot Wilson describes them, and it is terrific fun but where peal are concerned – whether fly fishing by night or plying a long line and a bait by day – the longer the rod you can handle comfortably under local circumstances the better you are equipped to bring your efforts to a successful conclusion.

Your purpose is to present a succulent worm to the quarry in as natural a way as possible without betraying your presence. The expression 'fine and far off' could have been coined with long-trotting in mind and apart from the obvious lightness of the end tackle and the line used the angler has to be in control throughout the passage of the baited hook down the currents to the fish. In this he is greatly assisted by a long rod and gravely hindered by a short one.

In fact, the keen coarse fisherman visiting the West Country may well have in his possession tackle more suitable for this purpose than many game fishermen who live close to the peal waters.

Way back through the mists of time a great friend and I would trot for the shy chub of the river Thames from a punt moored well above the fishes' holts under the roots of willow and alder. In those days, too, I watched two fishermen applying precisely the same tactics for sea trout from a punt stationed below the bridge at Christchurch on the river Avon. They used maggots, we used cheese or cheese paste and the only difference between what was done then and what we are talking about now is the bait and the fact that you are unlikely to fish from a punt! As far as the bait matters, we have already accepted maggots as deadly for peal and I can see no reason why they should not take cheese paste.

The rods used were between 12 and 14-ft, made of Spanish reed with a split cane top spliced to the reed of the top section. The reels were 4-in centre pins carrying 100 yards of 8-lb BS silk line, well anointed with a floatant. As the depth of the swim holding the chub was about 12 ft the cast of 3X gut was tailor-made for that depth and the float fixed just below the junction with the line.

To assist the fairly slow current of summertime Thames to carry the bait to the fish without undue delay the float was a long porcupine quill passed through the centre of a cork. To avoid float pressure – resistance to the chub when it took the cheese – the cast carried a fair load of shot to sink the cork almost entirely . . . and the top of the cork was shaved to streamline it against water resistance when the fisherman tightened into the fish!

Because the principles applying to trotting on Thames, Severn, Avon or any river are the same I should add that the shot load was fairly well dispersed along the cast. If you wish to fish a static bait on float tackle, then the weight should be concentrated at a point where it will lie on the bed of the river or lake, some twelve to eighteen inches from the hook. In trotting a bait over any distance of a stream where the bed is uneven it is best to have such shot as is required spread along the length of the cast: this allows the baited hook to rise in the water when checked against the current so that the angler can 'lift' it over obstacles.

Obviously there is considerable skill required to direct the end tackle to the desired spot. The current is used to steer the bait and to change its depth to conform with the uneven bottom and the value of a long rod cannot be stressed too much, while the assistance length gives in handling a good fish is worth considering. However, also bear in mind that moment when you need to bring the rod top back over your shoulder to draw the beaten trout over the landing net. Intervention by branches overhead can bring disaster instead of triumph and lead not only to a good fish lost, but a broken top as well.

When fishing for anything which demands the use of net or tailer, whether fishing with bait by day or fly by night, select your landing point in advance, choosing it both for convenience and as a place where the job can best be done without disturbing too much of the pool. You may even find a shelving gravel up which the fish can be beached without recourse to the net. My reference to a tailer refers to salmon alone: even grilse are better netted.

The weight or balance of your end tackle must depend solely on the conditions facing you at the riverside: but as far as float and shotting are concerned always work on the assumption that smaller and lighter is better. To this end it is often possible to run a bait down to a likely lie without the use of either and you are now employing the upstream worm in reverse – a practice which obviates the difficulty of casting, swinging or throwing the bait upstream, but may well increase the danger of betraying your presence to the fish.

The successful use of a worm fished upstream is an art form of its own and I doubt very much whether this method has ever been described better than it was by an old Edinburgh lawyer, W. C. Stewart, in his book *The Practical Angler* which was first published in 1857. In those days some of the fishermen this author met along the banks of those rivers of the Borders made a living with rod and line and developed their art to a niceness unlikely to be bettered by the modern anglers.

Again, this is a form of fishing which requires tackle and skills already acquired by coarse fishermen and offers the visitor idyllic hours of exploration and fishing along those miles of rivers where bait is allowed. For those who would sample this enjoyment it is unfortunate that the opportunity is restricted by the authority bye-laws. For example, no worms are allowed at any time on Avon, Exe or Taw and Torridge, while the use of the bait is banned on rivers Lyn and Teign before the beginning of June. Actually, that is the very time when worm fishing comes into its own and continues to provide the best of sport through that month and July. These two months follow the peak of fly fishing. On the Tamar and tributaries and all the Cornish rivers no holds are barred, except when decreed by owners or angling associations. In the waters controlled by the Wessex Water Authority no bait – prawn, shrimp or worm – may be used by persons fishing for salmon prior to May 15.

In Stewart's day and for that matter when first I fished the worm upstream to the small brownies of a local brook, a long rod was of utmost importance in enabling us to cast – a gentle, smooth swinging throw – the fairly fragile bait without tearing it from the hook. It is most advisable to have a supply of suitable worms which have been well scoured and hardened in advance of the fishing day. The long rod – between 12 and 14 feet – was also needed to give the angler control over his line as the bait came back towards him on the current. Today, although the fixed-spool reel has made it possible to cast happily enough with a shorter rod, the need for a long wand to control the bait and, for that matter, a hooked fish remains and the rods used by the float-fishing coarse fish angler are generally ideal for this purpose, just as they are for long-trotting.

A line to balance the rod is needed, but need not necessarily float since the length of the rod will enable the fisherman to keep in touch with his bait without allowing any loose line to sink. Of course, it is possible to find a worm under a stone, strip a fly of its feathers and tinsel and cast the bait with a fly rod and catch yourself a trout on a day when the fish refuse to rise! But here we are looking for the best tools to fit the task and it is a pleasant thought that our visitors can use the same outfit which suits the coarse fisheries of the Midlands and Home Counties for the purpose of extracting some of our sporting little brown trout.

In exceptional circumstances of deep strong water when the use of lead is essential to take the bait down to the trout before it is swept past them, worming should be as light a form of fishing as with the nymph: the worm is heavier than the fly, of course, but its presentation must be equally gentle. In the old days it was suggested that a length of line not more than the length of the rod and half as much again was ideal for both casting and fishing the worm back to the rod and, despite the angler's opportunity to cast the bait further on a fixed-spool reel, any greater distance is neither necessary nor desirable.

For my money this is a method best suited to fast and generally shallow runs in which the trout has taken up feeding stations, rather than in the deeper pools and holes below the bank where they have their holts: it is, too, associated with wading, for that is the ideal way of progressing up a river, with the ability to place the bait under either bank as well into those lies which exist further into the stream. An intimate knowledge of the river and the habits of the fish are obvious ingredients of success, but an ability to read the water will enable the most complete stranger to fish it with confidence and every chance of some success – a chance which grows the more often he fishes it!

Trout rarely feed where they rest anymore than do we – a fact which is often made obvious by the determined dash of a hooked fish towards its distant home.

With rather better intelligence of their environment than we possess the fish are able to take up station in the best places to intercept food brought to them by the current at a time when that food is expected. They can anticipate a hatch of fly and indulge themselves on the nymph or the imago during its occurrence, be it of short duration or throughout the day: but they also maintain their positions in the river (there is a definite pecking order so far as the best and most profitable spots are concerned – places occupied by trout of aldermanic proportions will quickly be filled by the next in line should the original holder of that tenancy make a sudden departure) when no fly are hatching, in the hope of intercepting other delicacies which may float down with the current, swim across the zone of vision or creep over the river bed.

It is to this end that you present your hook baited with the worm!

The ideal conditions for upstream fishing are provided by low, clear water – just about the opposite to the downstream methods already discussed for sea trout: although it cannot be stressed enough that a fast-flowing and dirty river offers no hope for any angler other than those who are content to drown a gob of lobworms anchored to a heavy lead.

Low clear water decrees the most cautious approach you can manage, whether in waders or on the bank. Wading reduces the stature and the distance from which the fish may detect you: bank fishing may demand some degree of fieldcraft accompanied by acute casting ability; but no matter how careful, how skilful you are, you are likely to frighten more fish than when fishing from the river and, consequently, catch fewer trout.

Some people, including myself, prefer to use a centre-pin reel. Throwing the worm to the head of the run or glide, where these are only small areas offering a lie to only one good trout or maybe two or three, you begin the retrieve with all line out and the rod fully extended in front of you. Raise the rod as the line comes back, and when at about 10 o'clock begin to collect the slack with one hand while that holding the rod is ready to tighten into a fish when it takes, signified by the line stopping or dipping to one side or other of the current.

If the worm is threaded head first up the hook and beyond the eye with a half inch of lively tail to wriggle beyond the bend, it is probable that the fish will seize the wriggly part and take the business end of the hook into its mouth. If the head is left free to move about at the other end or when two worms are impaled rather than one the fish may well attack a part well away from the business end of the hook. It is always preferable I think to use a bait in such a way as to enable an immediate strike: if nothing else I like to hook a fish before it is able to take the hook into its gullet, or miss it: I do not like the tricky task of using a disgorger to remove a deeply swallowed hook from a small or unwanted trout, or a smolt or salmon parr which will almost certainly not recover from the whole operation.

Your alternative is to tie up smaller hooks in tandem, even three and impale the worm on each along its body. With this little outfit you can happily make contact with your fish just as soon as it takes the bait. One snag, however, is the possibility that one or another of the hooks may hang free outside the fish's moth and become snagged into weed, a rock or some other submerged obstacle during the course of the ensuing struggle to the net.

Mentioning the net, I always carry one when wading, because at the height of the worming season there is always the chance of stumbling across a nice sea trout, even a grilse, although the general size of the brownies does not warrant the use of one. Sometimes in the shallower streams I know well a simple net on an oval frame and short handle suffices: at other times I prefer to combine the use of a long handle with net and wading staff, allowing it to trail the water behind me while fishing. With a biggish bass or bag tied to my belt on my other side to take the trout I kill, spare hooks, leader, knife, priest and disgorger in a pocket and a smaller bag to hold the worms, also tied to the belt in front of me I am fully equipped to fish as long as I wish to without leaving the river and by sticking the butt and reel into the top of a thigh boot can make both hands available to any task of unhooking fish and rebaiting the hooks.

A bonus of this method of fishing is that, although you will pick up the odd small trout, you tend to avoid bootlace eels and, so long as you avoid shallows, will not suffer too badly from voracious parr or, at that time of year, pick up unwanted smolts. In the earlier season the fly is more effective and to my mind always preferable for pure enjoyment, which is not to discount the skill required in upstream worming or the excitement and pleasure it affords.

APPENDIX 1

NATIONAL RIVERS AUTHORITY LICENCES

This list is as comprehensive as it can be at the time of publishing and shows the many agencies through which fishing licences can be obtained in the areas covered by South West and Wessex regions of the Authority. In many cases these distributors are also agents for the sale of permits on their own fisheries and others – both rivers and stillwaters. Many can provide the visitor with the latest news of sport and provide advice on local conditions and prospects as well as angling methods and tackle most likely to succeed.

South West

CORNWALL

Bodmin
Bodmin Trading Co., Church Square, PL31 2DP
R. Burrows, 26 Meadow Place, PL31 1JD
Combe Hill Leisure Ltd., Combe Hill, St. Breward, PL20 4LZ
P. Coppin, West End Garage, Higher Bore Street, PL31 1LZ
E. D. T. Jackson, Butterwell, Nanstallon, PL30 5LQ

Boscastle
North Cornwall Leisure, Lower Manor Meadows, Bude Road, PL35 0HF
The Wellington Hotel, The Harbour, PL35 0AQ

Bude
North Cornwall Pet & Garden Supplies, Princes Street

Callington
E. J. Dingle, Doney & Hancock, 26 Fore Street, PL17 7AD
The Stores, Rilla Mill, PL17 7NT

Camborne
Camborne Sporting Centre, 68 Union Street, TR14 8HF

Camelford
Camelford Gun Rooms, 4 Fore Street, PL32 9PE
Stephens & Son, 12 Market Place

Fowey
Fowey Marine Services, PL23 1DF
The Gift and Sports Shop, 10 Esplanade

Gunnislake
H. Symons, Lower Bealswood House

Launceston
Mr E. J. & Mrs D. M. Broad, Lower Dutson Farm
Mrs J. A. Chapman, Higher Bamham, PL15 9LD
Mrs T. D. Jonas, Cartha Martha, Rezare, PL15 9NX
Mike Summers Angling Centre, Unit 1, Southern Ct., Newport Ind. Est., PL15 8EX

Liskeard
The Fishing Tackle Shop, 13 Lower Lux Street, PL14 3JL
Liskeard & District Angling Club, Mr T. Sobey, Trevartha Farm, PL14 3NS
M. J. Peacock, Great Trethew Manor, Horning Tops, PL14 3PY
Trago Mills, Dobwalls
Godfreys Store, Barn Street

Looe
Looe Tropical & Pet Supplies, Buller Street, East Looe, PL14 1AS
Shillamill Lakes, Lanreath

95

Lostwithiel
R. W. Drayton, 28 North Street, PL22 0EF
The Earl of Chatham, Grenville Road, Bridgend

Newquay
Going Fishing, 32A Fore Street
Min-y-Don Hotel, Island Crescent
E. S. A. Mitchell, Trevella, Crantock, TR8 5EW
Newquay Fishing & Shooting Centre, 2 Beach Road, TR7 1ET
R. C. Penhaligon, 15 Queen Street

Otterham
St. Tinney Farm Holidays, PL32 9TA

Par
D & C Stores, 16 Harbour Road, PL24 2BB
Par Gift Shop, 105 Par Green

Penzance
Ken's Tackle, 26 Causeway Head, TR18 2SP
Newtown Angling Centre, The Shop, Newtown, Germoe
The Quay Shop, Quay Street
River Valley Caravan Park, Relubbus, Nr. Penzance
T. Shorland, Driftways, Drift Reservoir

Perranporth
Perran Sports, St Pirran's Road

St Austell
The Angling Centre, 10a Victoria Place
Innis Fish Farm, Innis Moor, Penwithick
Post Office, Roche
M.C. Fishing Tackle, 2 Market Hill

St Columb
St Columb Cycles, 52 Fore Street

Saltash
Notter Bridge Caravan & Camping Park, PL12 4RW

Wadebridge
Camel Firearms & Fishing, Unit 1, Chapel Lane
G. J. Dutton, G. Dutton Butchers, 25 Molesworth Street
N. J. Morton, 1 Egloshayle Road, PL27 6BX
Wadebridge Cycles & Fishing Tackle, Eddystone Road

Zelah
Venton Trissick Trout Farm, Zelah, Nr Truro, TR4 9DG

DEVON

Ashburton
The Church House Inn, Holne, Nr Ashburton, TQ13 7SJ
Holne Chase Hotel, TQ13 7NS
The Post Office, TQ13 7DD

Axminster
Axminster Sports, 4 Old Bell House, Trinity Square

Bampton
Exeter Inn, EX16 9DY

Barnstaple
The Kingfisher, 22 Castle Street
M. W. Maxse, Great Fisherton, Bishops Tawton, EX32 0ER
North Devon Angling Centre, 48 Bear Street, EX32 7DB
E.S.B. Wray, Pink Cottage, T/A Country Leisure Pursuits, Tawstock, EX31 3HZ

Beaworthy
W. H. B. Coham-Fleming, Coham, Black Torrington

Bideford
The Fishing Tackle Shop, 6 Grenville Street
Post Office Store, Weare Gifford, EX39 4QR
Torridge Fly Fishing Club, K. L. Parker, 4 Merryfield Road, EX39 4BX
The Tackle Box, Kings Shopping Centre, Cooper Street

Bovey Tracey
Glen Lyn Garage, Newton Road, TQ13 9DX

Brixham
Brixham Bait & Tackle, 12 Middle Street

Buckrfastleigh
Mabin News, 33 Fore Street, TQ 0AA

Budleigh Salterton
Budleigh Salterton Town Council, Enquiry Office, Public Hall, Station Road

Chagford
James Bowden & Sons, The Square, TQ13 8AH
Mill End Hotel, Sandy Park

Christow
The Teign House Inn, EX6 7PL

Chudleigh
Finlake Woodland Village, TQ13 0EJ

Chumleigh
Fox & Hounds Hotel, Eggesford, EX18 7JZ

Colyton
Wiscombe Park Fishery, Southleigh, EX13 6JE

NATIONAL RIVERS AUTHORITY LICENCES

Crediton
Ladds Gun and Sports, 86–87 High Street
Mrs H. A. Phillips, 144 High Street

Cullompton
County Sports, 3 Station Road, EX15 1AH
Hartsmoor Farm Fisheries, Clayhidon, EX1 5QB

Dawlish
Black Swan Angling Centre, 1A Piermont Place
Dawlish Sports, K & K Sports Ltd., 15 Brunswick Place

Drewsteignton
The Anglers Rest (Fingle Bridge) Ltd., The Anglers Rest, Fingle Bridge
Clifford Bridge Park, Clifford, EX6 6QE

Exeter
Brailey's Field Sports Centre, Market Street, EX1 1DW
Bridge Cafe and Stores, Countess Wear
Devon Sports Goods, 45 Cowick Street
Exeter Angling Centre, Smithen Street, Off Market Street, EX4 3JE
A. Gould, 47 Longbrook Street
Gun and Sport Shop, 76 Fore Street, Heavitree
P. K. Angling, 45 Clifden Road, EX1 2BJ
J. E. Rodway, Upexe Mill Farm, Thorverton, EX5 5NE

Exmouth
Exmouth Tackle Shop, 20 The Strand

Hatherleigh
Greenhills Newsagency, 6–8 Bridge Street, EX50 3HU
Miss E. Holl, Homelines, 41 Market Street

Holsworthy
Mrs M. Short, Langaton Farm, Whitstone, EX22 6TJ
Mr J. C. & Mrs M. Tidball, DIY Centre, 25 The Square
Woodford Bridge Hotel, Milton Damerel, EX22 7LH

Honiton
Combe House Hotel, Gittisham
Deer Park Hotel, Weston, EX14 0PG
T. D. Hussey & Son, Bank House, 66 High Street

Ilfracombe
Variety Sports Shop, 23 Broad Street, EX34 9EE

Ivybridge
'Erme Flies' Craft Centre, Mill Leat Trout Farm, Ermington
Pete Keenan Sports, 6 Glanville Mill
P. D. Bennett, The Gun Room, 5 Western Road

Kingsbridge
Loddiswell Post Office, Loddiswell, TQ7 4QH
Saddlery & Country Clothes, 55 Church Street, TQ7 1BT
Warden at Widdicombe Ley, Eight Bells, Beesands

Lynmouth
T. E. & K. Price, East Lyn House, Watersmeet Road, EX35 6SP

Lynton
Brendon House Hotel, Brendon, EX35 6PS
E. J. Pedder Newsagents, No. 1 Lee Road
Lyn Pet Supplies, Granville Houe, 13 Lee Road
Sunny Lyn Caravan & Camping Site, Lynbridge, EX35 6NS

Newton Abbot
E. R. Day, Wood House, Chudleigh
Drum Sports Limited, 47 Courtenay Street
Newton Abbot Angling Centre, 117 Queen Street, TQ12 2BG
Poundsgate Shop & Post Office, Poundsgate, TQ13 7NY
The River Dart Country Park, Holne Park, Ashburton, TQ13 7NP
Trago Mills, TQ12 6JD

Okehampton
Collavon Manor Hotel, Sourton, EX20 4HH
Mrs C. Fraser, 1 Bright View
Mr A. J. Short, T/A Geralds, 16–18 The Arcade, EX20 1EX
South Reed Fisheries, Boasley Cross, Bratton Clovelly, EX20 4J
Mrs C. W. Wickett, Richmond House, New Road, Merton, EX20 3EG

Ottery St Mary
Escot Aquaculture Ltd., Parklands Farm, Escot, EX11 1LU
Ottery Fly Fishing Club, M. D. Winter, 'Ottermead', 27 Oak Close

Paignton
J. E. Coombes, Avon Fishing Association, 19 Stella Road, Preston
The Sportsman, 7 Dartmouth Road, TQ4 5AB
SW Tackle Developments, 37 Church Street, TQ3 3AJ

Plymouth
Clives Tackle & Bait, 182 Exeter Street
D. K. Sports, South Devon House, 83 Vauxhall Street, Barbican
C. V. Osborne & A. S. Cragg, 37 Bretonside, PL4 0BB
The Tackle Box, 83 Exeter Street

Sheepwash
Half Moon Inn

Sidmouth
P. B. Coleman, Ottery Fishing Club, 1 Hazel Close, Newton Poppleford
The Small Boat Chandlers, Fore Street, EX10 8AH

South Molton
Castle Inn, Georgenympton
South Molton Sports Centre, 130 East Street

Tavistock
Endsleigh Fishing Club Ltd, Endsleigh, Milton Abbot
D. E. Rees, 15 Duke Street, PL19 0BB
Ayres Sport, 4 Pepper Street
Charles Bingham, Warrens Cross, Whitchurch PL19 9LD
J. Willis, The New Keep, 10 King Street

Teignmouth
Drakes Hotel, 33 Northumberland Place, TQ14 8UG

Tiverton
Bellbrook Valley Trout Fishery, Bellbrook Farm, Oakford, EX16 9EX
Bridge House Hotel, Bampton
Country Sports, 9 William Street
J. G. Martin, Essebeare, Witheridge, EX16 8QB
Tiverton Sports and Leisure, 4 Market Precinct

Torquay
Plainmoor Angling Centre, 141 St Marychurch Road, TQ1 1HW
The Sea Chest, 11 Torwood Street

Torrington
J. Gawesworth, Orford Lodge, EX38 8PH
Torrington Sports, 9 High Street, The Square

Totnes
Newhouse Fishery, Moreleigh, TQ9 7JS
Totnes Angling Centre, Unit 15, The Plains Shop Centre

Uffculme
Post Office, The Square, EX15 3AA

Umberleigh
Rising Sun Hotel, EX37 9DH

Westward Ho!
N. J. Laws, Summerlands, Golf Links Road

Winkleigh
Gp. Capt. P. Norton-Smith, Little Warham, Beaford

Withypool
Post Office & Stores, Nr Minehead, TA24 7QP

Yelverton
Badgers Holt Ltd., Dartmeet, PL20 6SG
J. D. Hamer, Rock Stores, Dousland Road, PL20 6AY
Prince Hall Hotel, Two Bridges
Princetown Post Office, Princetown, PL20 6QE
Post Office Store, Postbridge

SOMERSET

Chard
Chard Cycle Co., 16 Holyrood Street, TA20 2AH

Crewkerne
Sportsworld & Leisure, 31 Market Street

Dulverton
Anchor Inn, Exbridge, TA22 9AX
Carnarvon Arms Hotel, TA22 9AE
Lance Nicholson Fishing, 9 High Street
J. E. Sharpe, J. S. Sporting, Parlour Cottage, Hgr. Grants, Exbridge, TA22 9BE
Tarr Steps Hotel, Hawkridge, TA22 9PY

Minehead
Minehead Sports, 55 The Avenue, TA24 5DJ
Post Office Stores, Withypool TA24 7QP

Porlock
M. W. J. Williams, Lower Bourne House, High Street

Simonsbath
Exmoor Forest Hotel

Taunton
Enterprise Angling, 5 Silver Street
Topp Tackle, 61 Station Road, TA1 1PA

Wiveliscombe
Oxenleaze Farm Caravans, Chipstable, TA4 2QH

APPENDIX 2

LICENCE DISTRIBUTORS

AVON & DORSET AREA

Amesbury
Amesbury Abbey Nursing Home, Amesbury Abbey
Amesbury Post Office, Salisbury Street

Andover & District
Challis Gas, 60 Mylen Road
Cole & Son (Devizes) Ltd, 67 High Street
Specklebest Ltd, Keepers House, Fox, Amport, SP11 8BJ

Arthur Conyers Ltd (Gunmakers), West Street, Blandford, DT11 7AW

Bournemouth & District
Solar Sports, 174 Holdenhurst Road
Turbary Sports, Wonderhome Parade, Kinson Road
Throop Fishers, School House, Throop, BH8 0EF

Bat & Ball Public House, Salisbury Road, Breamore, Hants SP6 2EA

Bridport & District
The Sports Shop, 37 West Street
The Tackle Shop, West Bay Road, DT6 4EN
E.J. & M.R. Harris, Mangerton Mill, Mangerton, DT6 3SG

Aries Angling Centre, 11 The Precinct, Chandlers Ford

Christchurch
Davies Fishing Tackle, 75 Bargates, BH23 1QE
Pro Fishing Tackle, 2587 Barrack Road, BH23 2BJ

Dorchester & District
Specialist Angling Supplier, 1 Athelston Road, DT1 1NR
Sportarm (CW Building), Maumbury Road, DT1 1QW
Maiden Newton House, Maiden Newton

Fareham
Hansford's 55 Portland Street
Rovers Tackle Shop, 178b West Street

Fordingbridge & District
G. Debenham, East Mills Manor Estate, Southampton Road
Damerham Fisheries Ltd, Damerham, Southend
Sandy Balls Estate Ltd, Godshill
Rockbourne Trout Fisheries, Rockbourne SP6 1QG

Grayshott Tackle, 1 Crossways Road, Grayshott, Surrey BU26 6HJ

Mr. L. Daxter, St Mary's Pharmacy, The Square, Gillingham, Dorset SP8 4AS

N. V. Smith, Keeper's Cottage, Manor Farm Lane, Great Wishford, Wilts

Havant Angling Centre, 2 Park Way, Havant, Hants PO9 8HH

Tackle & Toys (South Coast Tackle), 7 Marine Parade West, Lee on Solent, PO13 9LL

Tropicana of Littlehampton, 6 Pier Road, Littlehampton BN17 5BA

Ron's Fishing Tackle, 465 Upper Richmond Road West, East Sheen, London SW 14

L & B Sheppard, Country Ways, 13 High Street, Luggershall, Hants

Marlborough & District
Leathercraft of Marlborough, Hughendon Yard, High Street, SN8 1LT
Savernake Forest Hotel, Burbage
Mrs R. Taylor, Lock House, Wootton Rivers

Spreadbury's, 28 High Street, Milford-on-Sea

Brig. A. G. Haywood, CBE, LVO, MC, Monkton House, Monkton Deverill

Field & Stream, 109 Bartholomew Street, Newbury

Bohune Farms, Manningford Bohune, Pewsey, SN9 6LY

99

Poole
Dick's Fishing Tackle, 66a High Street
Poole Angling Centre, 19 High Street
Wessex Water, 2 Nuffield Road

Portsmouth & District
Coombs Tackle Centre, 165 New Road, Copnor, PO2 7QS
Portsmouth & District Angling Society, 86 Carnarvon Road, Copnor

Ringwood & District
M. G. Pegler, 70 Wessex Road, BH24 1XE
Ringwood Tackle, 5 The Bridges, West Street
A. R. Warren, 'Quiet Water', Ivy Lane, Blashford

Creatures, 4 Market Place, Romsey, Hants

Rue Fisheries, Rue Farmhouse, Alweston, Nr Sherborne DT9 5JE

Salisbury & District
John Eadie (Sports & Fishing Tackle) 20 Catherine Street
The Rod Box, 20 Milford Street
Sheila's Station Care, South Western Road, SP2 7RR
Figheldean Post Office Stores, Figheldean, SP4 8JT
A. R. Hadley, Ladies Hairdressers, 129 The Borough, Downton
The Stag Inn, Charlton All Saints, SP5 4 HD
Teffont Fishing Club, Manor Cottage, Teffont Evias
F. E. & C. H. Crosier, Post Office, Tisbury, SP3 6LD
Hon A. D. Tryon, Kingfisher Mill, Great Dumford, SP4 6AY
J. H. & M. A. Reid Fishing Tackle, Kingway House, Wilton

Sport Equip, 37 High Street, Shaftesbury SP7 8JE

Southampton & District
Home Stores, 68 High Street, Swaythling, SO2 2HZ
Poingdestre's Angling Centre, 1–5 Cannon Street, Shirley, SO1 5PQ
Sports, Batt's Corner, 1a Rumbridge Street, Totton, SO4 4DQ

Sturminster Newton & District
Harts Garden Suppliers Ltd, Station Road
Stour Valley Sports, Market Cross
Corner Tackle Cottage, High Street Stalbridge

Swanage Angling Centre, 6 High Street, Swanage BH19 2NT

Pallington Lakes, Tincleton, Dorset
Wessex Fly Fishing, Lawrences Farm, Southover, Tolpuddle, DT12 7HF

Wareham
E. Elmes & Son, Ironmonger, 21 South Street
Guns & Sports, Practical Gunsmiths, 24 South Street

Warminster
AA Rod Angling Centre, 5 Chinns Court
Coates & Parker Ltd, 36 Market Place, BA12 9AN
Smith & Ford Sports (Warminster), 24 Three Horseshoes Mall

Weymouth & District
Angle Tackle Store, 64 Park Street
Osmington Mills Holidays Ltd, Crofters, Osmington Mills
Dennings, 114 Portland Road, Wyke Regis, DT4 9AD

Wimborne & District
Minster Sports, 8 West Street
Philinda Ltd, Whitesheet Lake, Whitesheet

Sparkes of Winchester, 95 Olivers Battery Road South, Winchester, SO22 4JQ

Woolbridge Manor Farm, Wool, Dorset

BRISTOL AVON AREA

Humberts Chartered Surveyors, Estate Office, Badminton, GL9 1DD

Bath & District
Fish-N-Shoot, 5 Cleveland Place East
Wessex Water, PO Bx 95, Quay House, The Ambury
T & T Tackle, 62 High Street, Midsomer Norton, BA3 2DQ
Newton Mill Touring Centre, Pennyquick, Newton St Loe, BA2 9SF
A. T. Veater & Sons, 1–2 Waldegrave Forecourt, Radstock, BS3 3AD

Bristol & District
Silver Dace Jnr AC, 4 Kenmore Drive, BS7 0TT
S. Veals & Son, 61 Old Market Street
Wessex Water, Passage Street, BS2 0JQ
Bristol Post Office Angling Club, 4 Friezewood Road, Ashton Gate, BS3 2AB
Severnside Tackle, 14 Meadow Street, Avonmouth, BS11 9AR
Talbot Tackle, 1 North Street, Bedminster, BS3 1EN
JB Sports Ltd, 5 Repton Road, Brislington

LICENCE DISTRIBUTORS

Bristol Waterworks Company, Woodford Lodge, Chew Stoke
A. T. Veater & Sons, 90 Cooks Hill, Clutton
Bitterwell Lake, The Chalet, Coapit Heath
Avon Valley Country Park, Pixash Lane, Bath Road, Keynsham, BS18 1ST
Chew Fly Fishing Club, 32 Old Vicarage Green, Keynsham, BS18 2DG
John & Janet Nix, Garden Centre, 5 Bath Hill, Keynsham
Bob's Pets, 410 Wells Road, Red Lion Hill, Knowle
B. Carver (Gents Hairdresser), High Street, Paulton
Pet & Garden Supplies, 4 Wootton Road, St Annes, BS4 4AL
Scott Tackles, 42 Soundwell Road, Staple Hill, BS16 4QP
Ship & Co (Fishing), 7 Victoria Street, Staple Hill
Bristol Angling Centre, 12 Doncaster Road, Southmead
Pet & Corn Stores, 14 The Plain, Thornbury
J. Hollister, 76 Station Road, Yate

Bradford Sports-n-Tackle, 17 Market Street, Bradford-on-Avon

Calne & District
T. K. Tackle, 123a London Road, SN11 0AG
Quemerford Gate Farm, Cherhill, SN11 8UL

Manor House Hotel, Castle Combe, SN14 7HR

Essex Tackle, 42 Goldsmith Road, Coronation Square, Cheltenham

Chippenham & District
Cole & Son (Devizes) Ltd, Sports Outfitters, 6 Market Place
Rob's Tackle, 22 Marshfield Road
Hinton Grange Hotel, Hinton, SN14 8HG
Mrs. P. M. Hillier, Upper Peckingell Farm, Langley Burrell
Ford Fly Fishers, Down Farm, Kington St. Michael

Harpers of Sodbury, 60 Broad Street, Chipping Sodbury

D & J Sports Ltd, 75 Cricklade Street, Cirencester, GL7 1HY

R. E. & O. W. Tovell, Prospect Post Office, 17 Lypiatt Road, Corsham

Devizes & District
Cole & Sons (Devizes) Ltd, 33 Market Place
Rod & Reel, 11 Sidmouth Street, SN10 1LD

D.R. & P.J. Hampton, Park Farm, Erlestoke
F.W. & B.E. Coleman, Mill Farm, Great Cheverell Lakeside, Rowde

Cheza Sports, 10 Kinghill Road, Dursley, GL11 4EJ

Turners Tackle and Bait, 4a Station Road, Faringdon, SN7 7BN

Frome Angling Centre, 11 Church Street, Frome, BA11 1PW

Lacock & District
Lacock Stores, 12 High Street, SN15 2LQ
A. J. Dann Esq, The River Bank, Reybridge, SN15 2PF

Malmesbury & District
Sport & Leisure, 36 High Street
R.G. & E.M. Baker, Southfield Farm, Great Mill Lane, Lea, SN16 9NF

Avon Angling and Sports Centre, 13 Bath Road, Melksham

Pet Lovers, 6 Bull Lane, Pill

Bateman's (Sports) Ltd, Kendrick Street, Stroud

Swindon & District
House of Angling, 50/60 Commercial Road
Swindon Angling Centre, 5 Shepphard Street
Cotswold Angling, Kennedys Garden Centre, Hyde Road, Kingsdown
Somerford Fishing Association, 81 The Circle, Pinehurst, SN2 1RF
Tredworth Fishing Tackle, 78 High Street, Tredworth, GL1 4SR

Trowbridge & District
Smith & Ford Sports (Trowbridge), Castle Street, BA14 8AF
Wessex Narrowboats, Hilperton Wharf, Canal Road, BA14 7RR
Wests of Trowbridge, 32 Roundstone Street
Fallow Down Fisheries (Leisure), 1 New Leaze, Steeple Ashton, BA14 6EF

Smith & Ford Sports (Westbury), High Street, Westbury

Cannon & Sons Sports Ltd, 34 High Street, Wootton Bassett, SN4 7AG

SOMERSET AREA

Flowers Farm Trout Lakes, Hilfield, Batcombe Down, DT2 7BA

St Quentin Road CCP, Bridgwater Road, Bathpool, TA2 8BG

Bristol Waterworks, Blagdon Lake, Blagdon, Bristol

Bridgwater & District
Bridgwater Angling Centre (Unit 1), Wye Avenue, Dunwear Estate
John's Tackle, 35 St John Street
SDM Sports & Leisure, 66 Eastover
The Beeches Carp Ponds, 8 Luxborough Road, Durleigh
Willow Barns, Newcotts Farm, North Newton, TA7 0DQ
Bridgwater Angling Association, 7 Webbers Way, Puriton, TA7 8AS

Burnham-on-Sea
The Burnham Tackle Box, 10 Regent Street, TA8 1AX
Burnham Tackle Centre, 29 Victoria Street, TA8 1AN
Holimarine Ltd, Marine Drive

Chard Cycle Company, 16 Holywood Street, Chard

Broadway House Caravan Park, Cheddar

Clevedon
In Sport, 12a Old Street, BS21 6NN
Latestop, 165 Old Church Road, BS21 7JB
Six Ways Sport, 4 Alexandra Road

Crewkerne Sportsworld and Leisure, 31 Market Street, Crewkerne, TA18 7JZ

Exeter Angling Centre, Smythen Street, Off Fore Street, Exeter EX1 1BN

Tor Guns & Tackle, 88 High Street, Glastonbury, BA6 9DZ

P. Thyer, 3 Church Street, Highbridge

Horner Tea Gardens, Horner, Nr Porlock, TA24 8HY

Ilchester Angling Centre, Northover, Ilchester

Langport Angling Centre, North Street, Langport

Southfork Caravan Park, Parrett Works, Martock, TA12 6AE

Stax, Townsend, Montacute, TA15 6XH

In Sport, 4 The Precinct, High Street, Portishead

E. Hobley & Son, Crowne Trading Estate, Shepton Mallet

Sporting Classics, 27 Cheap Street, Sherborne

Viaduct Trout Fishery, Cary Valley, Somerton, TA11 6LJ

H. R. Crombleholme, St James Street, South Petherton

Street Angling Centre, 160 High Street, Street

Taunton & District
Enterprise Angling, 5 Silver Street
Topp Tackle Shop, 61 Station Road
Glide & Son, Bushfurlong Farm, Isle Brewers, TA3 6QT

Plainmoor Angling Centre, 141 St Marychurch Road, Plainmoor, Torquay TQ1 3HW

Wellington Country Sports, 2 Brooks Place, High Street, Wellington

Weston Angling Centre, 25a Locking Road, Weston-super-Mare, BS23 3BY

D. J. Cox, Laburnam House, Sloway Lane, West Huntspill

Marney's Outfitting Ltd, 3 Bond Street, Yeovil, BA20 1PE

23 Fast-biting rudd demand concentration on a West Country reservoir.

24 Roy Buckingham, Chief Instructor at the Arundell Arms, throws a long line to sea trout on the hotel's stretch of the Lyd.

25 Members of Bodmin Anglers' Association at work building a section of a weir. Steel rods are driven into the bedrock, large stones piled between them and the whole structure held together with mortar.

26 Two limit bags of wild brown trout caught from Colliford Lake – a natural brown trout water.

27 Low water on the Windrush – Asthall Water. (*Photo: David Reinger*)

28 The Penpont at Altarnun, a small but important salmon nursery for the rivers Inny and Tamar.

29 Chris Lobb of Silverton casting on the Middle Pool at Innis Moor, near St Austell

30 Eddy Chambers with a 20 lb pike caught at Slapton Ley. (*Photo: E. Chambers*).

APPENDIX 3

FISHING SEASONS

National Rivers Authority: South West Region

The 'Open Seasons', i.e. the period when it is permitted to fish are:

Species of Fish	Fishery District	Major Rivers within District	Rod & Line Open Season (dates inc.) Commences	Finishes
Salmon	Avon	Avon	15 Apr	30 Nov E
		Erme	15 Mar	31 Oct
	Axe	Axe, Lim, Otter, Sid	15 Mar	31 Oct
	Camel	Camel	1 Apr	15 Dec
	Dart	Dart	1 Feb	30 Sept E
	Exe	Exe	14 Feb	30 Sept
	Fowey	Fowey, Looe, Seaton	1 Apr	15 Dec
	Tamar & Plym	Tamar, Tavy, Lynher	1 Mar	14 Oct
		Plym	1 April	15 Dec
		Yealm	1 Apr	15 Dec E
	Taw & Torridge	Taw, Torridge	1 Mar	30 Sept
		Lyn	1 Feb	31 Oct
	Teign	Teign	1 Feb	30 Sept
Migratory Trout	Avon	Avon	15 Apr	30 Sept
		Erme	15 Mar	30 Sept
	Axe	Axe, Lim, Otter, Sid	15 Apr	31 Oct
	Camel	Camel, Gannel, Menalhyl, Valency	1 Apr	30 Sept
	Dart	Dart	15 Mar	30 Sept
	Exe	Exe	15 Mar	30 Sept
	Fowey	Fowey, Looe, Seaton, Tresillian	1 Apr	30 Sept
	Tamar & Plym	Tamar, Lynher, Plym, Tavy, Yealm	3 Mar	30 Sept
	Taw & Torridge	Taw, Torridge, Lyn	15 Mar	30 Sept
	Teign	Teign, Bovey	15 Mar	12 Oct

Species of Fish	Fishery District	Major Rivers within District	Rod & Line Open Season (dates inc.) Commences	Finishes
Brown Trout	Entire Region	R. Camel & R. Fowey	1 Apr	30 Sept
		Other Rivers & Streams	15 Mar	30 Sept
		All Other Waters	15 Mar	12 Oct
Rainbow Trout		ENTIRE REGION	NO CLOSE SEASON	
Coarse Fish		ENTIRE REGION	NO CLOSE SEASON	

As part of the Authority's Strategy on Salmon Cropping, the season on some rivers has been changed experimentally and is indicated with an E.
NOTE Some waters are not open for the full duration of the season, anglers are advised to check with the fishery owner if in doubt.

National Rivers Authority: Wessex Region

Coarse fishing does have a close season and fishing is allowed from 16 June to 14 March inclusive: there is, however, no close season for rainbow trout. These rules apply to rivers and stillwaters.

ANNUAL CLOSE SEASON
Salmon Bristol Avon & Somerset areas fishing is allowed from 1 February to 30 September.
Avon & Dorset area rod fishing on Frome and Piddle from 1 March to 30 September: elsewhere from 1 February to 30 September.

Migratory Trout Throughout entire region fishing is permitted 15 April to 31 October

Non-migratory Trout Fishing season from 1 April to 15 October in all rivers and from 17 March to 15 October in reservoirs, lakes and ponds throughout the region: but the start to the season is put back to 15 April on the Hampshire Avon and its tributaries above Mill Dam at Bickton Mill and the Nadder above Barford St Martin.

APPENDIX 4

ROD LICENCE DUTIES 1991

National Rivers Authority, South West Region, Manley House, Kestrel Way, Sowton, Exeter EX2 7LQ. Tel: 0392–444000

		Full £	Concession £
Salmon and Sea Trout:	Annual	35.00	17.50
	Week	17.50	8.75
	Day	4.50	2.25
Trout	Annual	8.80	4.40
	Week	4.50	–
	Day	2.00	1.00
Freshwater	Annual	2.60	1.30
	Week	1.00	–

Concessions: The following are eligible for concession fishing licences; documents accepted as proof of eligibility are also listed: OAPS: State Retirement Pension Book; Children under 16: Birth Certificate; Students under 18 in full-time education: Student Union Card or Certificate from Head of Education Establishment and Birth Certificate; Registered Disabled Persons: Certificate of Registration DP21 (green card) issued under the Disabled Persons (Employment Act) 1944 and 1958 or in receipt of a State Disability Pension or Mobility Allowance.

National Rivers Authority, Wessex Region, Rivers House, East Quay, Bridgwater, Somerset TA6 4YS. Tel: 0278–457333

	ANNUAL Adult £	Junior £	WEEKLY Adult £	Junior £
Salmon (inc trout, freshwater fish and eels)	37.00	18.50	6.00	3.00
Trout	11.50	5.75	2.80	1.40
Freshwater Fish (Coarse) and eels	8.80	4.40	2.20	1.10

Day Block: £1.40 per person

Second Rod: Supplementary fee payable for use of a second rod when fishing for freshwater fish – £1.00

Notes
1. All licences will apply to the whole of the Authority's fisheries area.
2. A Rod Licence must be taken out at the age of 12 years. Junior Licences will be available up to the age of 16 years.
3. Annual Rod Licences at the Junior rate will also be available to Old Age Pensioners and Registered Disabled persons.
4. The Daily Block Licence for freshwater fish and eels will be available to parties of 12 or more named persons fishing on one day only.

APPENDIX 5

FISHING CHARGES 1991

SOUTH WEST WATER PLC, Reservoir Fishing Charges
Prices include NRA Licence

Stocked Brown Trout Fishery
Fernworthy: Season 27 April to 12 October
Bag limits: Adult 4 fish,
Child 2 fish, Evening 2 fish

	£		£
Day:	12.50	Season	460.00
Concession:	10.50	Season	360.00
Child under 16:	3.50	Season	125.00
Evening:	7.50		

Stocked Rainbow Fisheries
Kennick, Siblyback: Season 29 March to 31 October. Start may vary to suit Easter
Wimbleball: Season 19 April to 31 October
Argal: Season 29 March to 31 October (boat only 1 June to 14 September inclusive)
Bag limits: Adult 6 fish day and concession, Child 2 fish, Evening 3 fish.

Day:	10.50
Concession:	8.50
Child under 16:	2.50
Evening:	6.50

Prepaid-permits available for stocked trout. Individuals or groups of anglers may purchase. Blocks of 10 permits available at 10% discount and blocks of 20 at 15% discount. For stocked trout anglers who fish frequently, non transferable blocks of 40 permits of day or day/evening combination are available at 20% discount.

Boat Prices

	Day £	Half day £
Siblyback, Kennick	6.00	4.50
Argal, Fernworthy	5.00	3.50
Wimbleball	5.00	–

Budget Trout Fisheries
Wistlandpound, Upper Tamar, Burrator, Stithians, Crowdy
Season: 15 March to 12 October
Bag limit: 4 fish

		£		£
Castabout Season;		75.00		
Day:	5.00	Season	65.00
Concession:	3.00	Season:	40.00
Child:	1.50	Season:	15.00

Natural Brown Trout Fishery
Colliford
Season: 15 March to 12 October
Bag limit: 4 fish

Day:	6.50	Season:	85.00
Concession:	4.00	Season:	52.00
Child:	1.50	Season:	15.00

Concessions: these reduced priced permits are for OAPs, holders of State Disability Pension or Mobility Allowance, and for full-time students under 18 years of age.

FISHING CHARGES 1991

BRISTOL WATERWORKS COMPANY

	£			£
Season 'A': All Waters Full:	420.00	*Season 'C': Chew/Barrow* Full:		320.00
OAP R/D (weekdays only):	252.00	OAP (weekdays only):		192.00
Junior:	185.00	Junior:		144.00

Season 'B': Barrow only Full: 200.00
OAP (weekdays only): 120.00
Junior: 90.00

Day Bank

	£			£			£
All Waters Full:	10.00	Chew/Barrows Full:	8.00	Barrow	Full:	6.50
OAP, R/D:	8.00	OAP, R/D:	6.00		OAP, R/D:	5.00
Junior:	5.00	Junior:	4.00		Junior:	3.50
		Chew 3pm:	5.50			

Day Boat

	£			£
Chew Full:	22.50	Blagdon Full:		18.50
OAP, R/D:	20.50	OAP, R/D:		16.50
Junior:	19.00	Junior:		15.50
3pm:	14.00	3pm:		12.00

Bag limits: day permit 8 fish, Chew evening permit 4 fish.
Anglers on these reservoirs also require an NRA (Wessex Region) Trout Licence

WESSEX WATER PLC, Stocked Trout Fisheries
Prices include NRA Licence

Reservoir	*Opening Date*	*Full Permit*	*Concession Permit*
		£	£
Sutton Bingham	23 March 1991	250.00	200.00
Clatworthy	16 March 1991	250.00	200.00
Hawkridge	16 March 1991	250.00	200.00
Otterhead	16 March 1991	225.00	175.00

Concessionary prices are available to OAP's, Juniors under 16 and registered disabled persons.

Permit Charges	*Full Permit*	*Concession Permit*
	£	£
Day Bank	9.50	7.50
Durleigh Only	9.00	–
Boat Charges	8.00	–

Boat charge with electric motor only available at Sutton Bingham: £13.00. *Boat* after 16.00 hrs: £5.00.

Bag Limits: Day Ticket 5; Season Ticket 4; Junior Ticket 2 (£3.00); Evening Ticket 2 (£5.00), Sutton Bingham and Clatworthy only.

APPENDIX 6

PENINSULA COARSE FISHERIES

BOSCATHNOE, PENZANCE
Water	4 acre reservoir
Species	Carp, tench, bream, roach, rudd and perch
Permits	Ken's Tackle, 9 Beachfield Court, The Promenade, Penzance, Tel: 0736–61969
	Lanxon's Sports, 18 Causewayhead, Penzance, Tel: 0736–62736
	Newton Angling Centre, Germoe, Tel: 0736–763721
Charges:	Per day £2.50; OAPs, SDP/MOB, students and children under 16 £1.50; 7 day Castabout, Full £15.00, Concession £10
	No Season Permits
Season and Times:	Open all year, 1 hour before sunrise to 1 hour after sunset

BUSSOW, ST IVES
Water:	7 acre reservoir
Species:	Carp, tench, bream, rudd and roach
Permits:	Ken's Tackle, 9 Beachfield Court, The Promenade, Penzance, Tel: 0736–61969
	Lanxon's Sports, 18 Causewayhead, Penzance, Tel: 0736–62736
	The Shirehorse Inn, Towednack Road, Hellesveor, St Ives, Tel: 0736–796724
	Newton Angling Centre, Germoe, Tel: 0736–763721
Charges:	Per day £2.50; 24 hour £5; OAP's, SDP/MOB, students and children under 16 £1.50; 7 day Castabout, Full £15.00, Concession £10.00; 7 day Castabout day and night £30.00
	No Season Permits
Season and Times:	Open all year, 24 hours per day

COLLEGE RESERVOIR, FALMOUTH
Water:	38 acre reservoir
Species:	Carp, tench, bream, rudd, roach and perch
Permits:	Day and night permits from self service unit at Argal car park
	Season Permits from the Ranger
	Day Permits – Ken's Tackle, 9 Beachfield Court, The Promenade, Penzance, Tel: 0736–61969
	Newton Angling Centre, Germoe, Tel: 0736–763721
Charges:	Per season: Castabout (day and night) £67.50; (Day) £45.00; OAPs, SDP/MOB £30.00; Children under 16 £15.00. Per day: £3.00; 24 hour £6.00; OAPs SDP/MOB, students £2.00; Children under 16 £1.50; 7 day Castabout, Full £15.00, Concession £10.00; 7 day Castabout day and night £30.00
Season and Times:	Open all year, 24 hours a day
Contact:	Bob Evans, Ranger, Little Argal Farm, Budock, Penryn, Tel: 0326–72544

CRAFTHOLE, SALTASH
Water: 2 acre lake
Species: Carp and tench
Permits: Mr Rogers, Post Office Store, Crafthole, St Germans, Saltash (open 0700 to 1300, 1400 to 1730; Sundays 0800 to 1215), Tel: 0503–30225
Charges: Per day £3.00; OAPs, SDP/MOB, students £2.00; Children £1.50 (must be accompanied by an adult). No Season Permits
Season and Times: Open all year, 1 hour before sunrise to 1 hour after sunset

JENNETTS, BIDEFORD
Water: 8 acre reservoir
Species: Carp, tench, roach, bream
Permits: The Tackle Box, Unit 5, Kings Shopping Centre, Cooper Street, Bideford, North Devon, Tel: 0237–470043 (Closed on Sundays)
Charges: Per day £3.00; OAPs, SDP/MOB, Students £2.00; Children £1.50
Season and Times: Open all year, 6.30 am to 10.00 pm

LOWER TAMAR LAKE, BUDE
Water: 40 acre lake
Species: Carp, tench, bream, rudd and roach
Permits: Day and night permits from self service unit at Lower Tamar lake car park. Season permits from Ranger at Upper Tamar Lake
Charges: Per season: Castabout (day and night) £67.50, (Day) £45.00; OAPs, SDP/MOB £30.00; Children under 16 £15.00. Per day £3.00; 24 hour £6.00; OAPs, SDP/MOB, students £2.00; Children under 16 £1.50; 7 day Castabout, Full £15.00; Concession £10.00; 7 day Castabout day and night £30.00
Season and Times: Open all year, 24 hours a day
Contact: Ranger at Upper Tamar Lake, Tel: 028882–262

MELBURY, PARKHAM, NR BIDEFORD
Water: 12 acre reservoir
Species: Carp, tench, bream, roach
Permits: The Tackle Box, Unit 5, Kings Shopping Centre, Cooper Street, Bideford, North Devon, Tel: 0237–470043
Powlers Piece Garage, Powlers Piece, East Putford, Tel: 02375–282
Summerlands Tackle, 3 Golflinks Road, Westward Ho!, Tel: 0237–471291
Charges: Per day £2.50; OAPs, SDP/MOB, Students and children under 16 £1.50; 7 Day Castabout, Full £15.00, Concession £10.00
Season and Times: Open all year, 6.30 am to 10.00 pm

OLD MILL, DARTMOUTH
Water: 4.67 acre reservoir
Species: Carp, tench, bream, roach
Permits: The Sport'n'Fish, 16 Fairfax Place, Dartmouth, Tel: 0803–833509
Charges: Per day £2.50; 24 hour £5.00; OAPs, SDP/MOB, students and children under 16 £1.50; 7 day Castabout, Full £15.00, Concession £10.00; 7 day Castabout day and night £30.00. No Season Permits
Season and Times: Open all year, 24 hours per day

PORTH RESERVOIR, NEWQUAY

Water: 40 acre reservoir
Species: Carp, tench, bream, rudd, roach and perch
Permits: Day and night permits from self service unit at Porth car park
Season Permits from Mrs P Ford, The Bungalow, Porth Reservoir, Tel: 0637–879481
Day Permits – Ken's Tackle, 9 Beachfield Court, The Promenade, Penzance, Cornwall, Tel: 0736–61969
Newton Angling Centre, Germoe, Tel: 0736–763721
Charges: Per season: Castabout (day and night) £67.50, (Day) £45.00; OAPs, SDP/MOB £30.00; Children under 16 £15.00. Per day: £3.00; 24 hour £6.00; OAPs, SDP/MOB, students £2.00; Children under 16 £1.50; 7 day Castabout, Full £15.00, Concession £10.00; 7 day Castabout day and night £30.00
Season and Times: Open all year, 24 hours a day
Contact: Mrs P. Ford at Porth Reservoir

SLADE RESERVOIRS, ILFRACOMBE

Water: Upper Slade 4 acres, Lower Slade 6 acres
Species: Carp, tench, bream, roach, perch and gudgeon
Permits: The Post Office, Slade, Tel: 0271–862257
The Tackle Box, 2b Portland Street, Ilfracombe, Tel: 0271–862570
The Kingfisher, 22 Castle Street, Barnstaple, Tel: 0271–44919
Summerlands Tackle, 3 Golflinks Road, Westward Ho!, Tel: 0237–471291
Charges: Season: Day and Night £56.00; Day only £37.00; OAPs, SDP/MOB and Students £20.00; Children under 16 £12.50. 24 hour: £5.00; OAPs, SDP/MOB, students and children under 16 £1.50; 7 day Castabout, Full £15.00, Concession £10; 7 day Castabout day and night £30.00
Season and Times: Open all year, 24 hours per day

SQUABMOOR, BUDLEIGH SALTERTON

Water: 4.3 acre reservoir
Species: Carp, tench, bream, rudd, roach
Permits: The Post Office, Knowle. The Tackle Shop, 20 The Strand, Exmouth. Exeter Angling Centre, Smythen Street, Exeter
Charges: Season: Day and Night £56.00; Day only £37.00; OAPs, SDP/MOB and students £20.00; Children under 16 £12.50. Per day: £2.50; 24 hour £5; OAPs, SDP/MOB, students and children under 16 £1.50; 7 day Castabout, Full £15.00, Concession £10.00; 7 day Castabout day and night £30.00
Season and Times: Open all year, 24 hours per day

TRENCHFORD RESERVOIR PIKE FISHERY, BOVEY TRACEY

Water: 45 acre reservoir
Species: Pike up to 30 lb
Permits: Self-service unit at Kennick Reservoir
Charges: Per day £2.50; OAPs, SDP/MOB, students, children under 16 £1.50
Season and Times: 1 October to 14 March inclusive, 1 hour before sunrise to 1 hour after sunset
Methods: Spinner, plug, worm or dead sea fish

APPENDIX 7

ANALYSIS OF ROD AND TROUT CATCHES 1989

Table 1: RODS, 1989 CATCHES AND WEIGHTS

River	Salmon No.	Weight (lb)	Sea Trout No.	Weight (lb)
Avon	65	446	255	388
Axe	0	0	90	96
Camel	244	1833	369	520
Dart	128	1048	502	1132
Erme	6	30	23	39
Exe	331	1969	9	10
Fowey	149	1014	472	587
Looe	2	14	103	118
Lyn	206	987	72	179
Lynher	15	111	213	359
Otter	0	0	42	54
Plym	18	185	144	236
Seaton	1	8	4	7
Tamar	344	2431	276	296
Tavy	38	250	214	294
Taw	160	1322	204	514
Teign	136	1106	565	974
Torridge	29	222	44	99
Tresillian	0	0	2	2
Valency	–	–	–	–
Yealm	1	6	43	78
Hayle	0	0	5	6
Other	0	0	2	2
Total	1873	12982	3653	5990

TABLE 2 : RODS, 1989 MONTHLY SALMON CATCHES

River	Feb	Mar	Apr	May	Jun	Jul	Aug	Sep	Oct	Nov	Dec	Unsp*	Total
Avon			0	0	0	0	0	13	20	32			65
Camel			0	3	7	8	13	46	50	79	38		244
Dart	2	4	21	14	10	4	11	57					123
Erme		0	0	0	0	0	1	1	4				6
Exe		25	22	7	26	28	13	210					331
Fowey			0	3	2	2	3	13	26	78	22		149
Looe			0	0	0	1	0		0	1	0		2
Lyn	0		6	3	28	41	67	25	36				206
Lynher		1	0	2	2	1	4	4	1				15
Plym		0	0	0	0	0	0	0	1	8	9		18
Tamar		6	36	38	27	21	16	153	47				344
Tavy		0	0	0	0	1	2	23	12				38
Taw		37	31	24	10	4	0	54					160
Teign	6	15	17	8	15	12	26	35	2				136
Torridge		4	11	2	1	0	1	10					29
Valency			0	0	0	0	0	0	0		0		
Seaton											1		1
Yealm										1			1
Total	8	92	144	104	128	123	157	644	199	199	70		1868

* Unspecified Month

TABLE 3: RODS, 1989 MONTHLY SEA TROUT CATCHES

River	Mar	Apr	May	Jun	Jul	Aug	Sep	Oct	Unsp*	Total
Avon		0	3	32	105	53	62	0		255
Axe		2	24	6	16	19	12	11		90
Camel		0	31	87	109	84	56	1	1	369
Dart	0	17	100	109	76	95	107			502
Erme	0	0	0	0	6	13	3	1		23
Exe	0	0	0	0	6	0	3			9
Fowey		3	12	67	187	126	77	0		472
Looe		0	5	15	42	34	7			103
Lyn		0	0	17	27	19	8	1		72
Lynher	1	5	20	50	72	47	18	0		213
Otter		0	1	2	4	13	12	0		42
Plym	2	5	7	26	57	26	19	2		144
Tamar	1	1	2	26	158	22	64	2		276
Tavy	2	2	10	20	76	41	63	0		214
Taw	1	21	31	43	25	31	52			204
Teign	2	7	32	93	142	92	170	27		565
Torridge	0	0	11	13	6	7	7			44
Yealm	0	0	0	1	21	12	9			43
Others	0	0	0	0		2				2
Tres.	0	0	0	0	1	1				2
Seaton					2		1		1	4
Hayle		5								5
Total	9	68	289	605	1138	737	750	55	2	3653

*Unspecified month
Others = Seaton, Tresillian.

TABLE 4: RODS, 1989 SALMON CATCHES COMPARED WITH PREVIOUS SEASONS

River		1989	1980	1981	1982	1983	1984	1985	1986	1987	1988
Avon	(a)		15	19							
	(b)	65	15	19	12	7	17	19	49	53	71
Axe	(a)		7	6							
	(b)	0	7	6	3	1	1	0	0	0	0
Camel	(a)		230	236							
	(b)	244	197	200	177	214	194	153	222	198	556
Dart	(a)		198	172							
	(b)	123	161	162	115	188	91	344	455	188	394
Erme	(a)		16	8							
	(b)	6	12	4	1	0	0	0	2	0	3
Exe	(a)		423	437							
	(b)	331	384	394	252	341	292	707	672	824	1030
Fowey	(a)		397	297							
	(b)	149	368	282	131	114	277	224	286	300	388
Looe	(a)		2	0							
	(b)	2	2	0	1	1	3	2	2	2	3
Lyn	(a)		71	91							
	(b)	206	65	82	69	82	41	110	130	94	110
Lynher	(a)		118	98							
	(b)	15	116	95	78	68	46	95	160	113	153
Plym	(a)		32	29							
	(b)	18	32	21	42	19	58	8	19	14	26
Tamar	(a)		1169	1109							
	(b)	344	1063	963	292	357	373	814	893	478	787
Tavy	(a)		110	123							
	(b)	38	92	116	50	28	43	170	134	99	267
Taw	(a)		795	412							
	(b)	160	680	387	192	197	101	320	416	155	381
Teign	(a)		81	93							
	(b)	136	72	92	93	145	73	128	258	143	303
Torridge	(a)		196	154							
	(b)	29	154	130	46	53	41	57	65	30	106
Yealm	(a)		1	4							
	(b)	1	1	4	5	1	1	2	0	0	0
Others	(a)		0	1							
	(b)	1	0	0	2	0	0	0	0	0	1
Total	(a)		3861	3289							
	(b)	1868	3421	2957	1661	1816	1652	3173	3763	2691	4579

(a) With reminders   (b) Unprompted

APPENDIX 7

TABLE 5 : RODS 1989 SEA TROUT CATCHES COMPARED WITH PREVIOUS SEASONS

River		1989	1980	1981	1982	1983	1984	1985	1986	1987	1988
Avon	(a)		93	354							
	(b)	255	90	328	167	155	76	96	160	277	213
Axe	(a)		77	142							
	(b)	90	63	120	31	28	38	24	36	129	98
Camel	(a)		632	1484							
	(b)	369	577	1326	1278	1189	687	451	572	1451	1118
Dart	(a)		343	570							
	(b)	502	261	539	770	545	437	283	149	631	683
Erme	(a)		57	99							
	(b)	23	39	50	52	19	7	46	35	24	60
Exe	(a)		5	14							
	(b)	9	5	4	32	17	5	9	6	15	10
Fowey	(a)		1016	2493							
	(b)	472	904	2179	985	1512	782	804	968	1762	1541
Looe	(a)		42	127							
	(b)	103	28	114	95	136	67	165	91	186	101
Lyn	(a)		70	68							
	(b)	72	68	63	122	65	51	172	92	66	137
Lynher	(a)		281	376							
	(b)	213	264	337	207	234	236	185	158	374	369
Otter	(a)		63	119							
	(b)	42	57	98	67	65	25	13	9	66	53
Plym	(a)		294	838							
	(b)	144	280	749	555	618	332	316	289	363	322
Tamar	(a)		352	1105							
	(b)	276	333	905	777	724	336	362	320	843	597
Tavy	(a)		408	676							
	(b)	214	340	601	517	558	295	206	308	706	525
Taw	(a)		1247	1082							
	(b)	204	1026	810	820	838	592	458	583	1437	645
Teign	(a)		875	2158							
	(b)	565	671	1972	1965	1359	944	1056	1419	1841	953
Torridge	(a)		633	424							
	(b)	44	464	378	464	329	60	108	349	633	226
Yealm	(a)		11	106							
	(b)	43	11	106	37	44	39	40	56	33	73
Others	(a)		19	116							
	(b)	13	19	114	71	113	32	44	56	61	31
Total	(a)		6518	12351							
	(b)	3653	5500	10793	9012	8548	5041	4838	5656	10898	7755

(a) With reminders (b) Unprompted

TABLE 6 : RODS 1954–1989, SALMON AND SEA TROUT CATCH ANALYSES 1954–1989

| | Salmon ||| Sea Trout |||
River	Lowest	Average	Highest	Lowest	Average	Highest
Avon	(c)	(c) 24	(c) 71*	(c) 61	(c) 178	(c) 354
Axe		18	71	24	95	254
Camel	36	235	556*	186	1151	2580
Dart	47	233	475	65	695	1496
Erme	(c) 0	(b)	(c) 16	(c) 7	(c) 54	(c) 110
Exe	48	715	2055	0	18	101
Fowey	43	210	483	616	1467	2804
Looe	(a) 0	(b)	(a) 3	(a) 42	(a) 135	(a) 332
Lyn	20	128	414	17	106	599
Lynher	13	86	260	54	243	451
Otter	–	–	–	2	61	216
Plym	0	21	157	68	264	838
Tamar	163	589	1169	134	430	1105
Tavy	28	109	267*	206	792	1672
Taw	101	419	971	437	1390	3726
Teign	40	111	303*	460	1163	2226
Torridge	29	286	883	60	878	2506
Yealm	(a) 0	(b)	(b) 5	3	37	106
Others	0	(e)	(d) 710	0	(e)	(d) 1502

(a) 1959–1989 only
(b) Insufficient data for long-term averages to be calculated.
(c) 1974–1989 data only.
(d) Including fish unspecified on 'Universal Licence' returns.
(e) Not applicable.
* 1988

APPENDIX 8

SOME USEFUL CONTACTS

NATIONAL RIVERS AUTHORITY

Wessex Region
Headquarters and Somerset area Rivers House, East Quay, Bridgewater. Tel: Bridgewater 45733
Bristol Avon area Tel: Bath 444066.
Avon & Dorset area Tel: Blandford 456080.

South West Region
Headquarters and East area Manley House, Kestrel Way, Exeter. Tel: Exeter 444000.
West area Tel: Bodmin 78301.

WATER COMPANY FISHERIES

Bristol Water
For general information about fly fishing at Chew, Blagdon and the Barrows, contact Woodford Lodge, Chew Stoke on Bristol 332339.

Wessex Water
For general information telephone Bristol 290611, or the following:
  Ivan Tinsley on Yetminster 872389 for *Sutton Bingham*
  Dave Pursey on Wiveliscombe 23549 for *Clatworthy*
  Gary Howe on Bridgewater 424786 for *Durleigh, Hawkridge, Otterhead*.

South West Water
For general information telephone Exeter 219666, or the following:
  Bob Evans on Falmouth 72544 for *Argal* and *Stithians*
  Reg England on Liskeard 42366 for *Siblyback* and *Colliford*
  Louise Sims on Bude 82262 for *Crowdy* and *Upper Tamar*
  Bob Lunk on Brompton Regis 372 for *Wimbleball* and *Wistlandpound*
  David Long on 0647 432440 for *Fernworthy, Kennick, Avon dam, Burrator* and *Venford*
  Ken Spalding on Bratton Clovelly 534 for *Meldon* (and eventually *Roadford*)

Peninsula Coarse Fisheries in general: contact the manger Dell Mills on Liskeard 43929.

The latest information about the above fisheries is available in booklet form from the Headquarters addresses shown.

BIBLIOGRAPHY AND RECOMMENDED READING

West Country Fly Fishing (edited Anne Voss Bark), Batsford, 1983
Salmon Fishing, W. Earl Hodgson, A. C. Black, 1927
Clear Waters, A. G. Bradley, Constable & Company, 1915
The Trout are Rising, B. Bennion, Bodley Head, 1920
The Practical Angler, W. C. Stewart, A & C Black, 1857
Stillwaters Trout, John Mitchell, Pelham Books Ltd, 1987
Fishing Flies and their Plumage, Michael Veale, Sportsman's Press, 1989
Sea Trout Run, Peter Jarrams, A & C Black, 1987
Salmon and Sea Trout Fishing, Charles Bingham, Batsford, 1988
River Trout Fly Fishing, Peter Lapsley, Unwin Hyman, 1988

Note: While Peter Jarrams' book has absolutely no connection with the sea trout or peal of the West Country, they are all one and the same animal whether known as whitling, white fish, sewin or whatever and the reader new to the species will find much of interest in its pages. The works by Peter Lapsley and Charles Bingham can provide the would-be river fisherman with all he needs to know about the catching of salmon and trout ... that is to the threshold of personal experience.

Principal Rivers of the South West of England

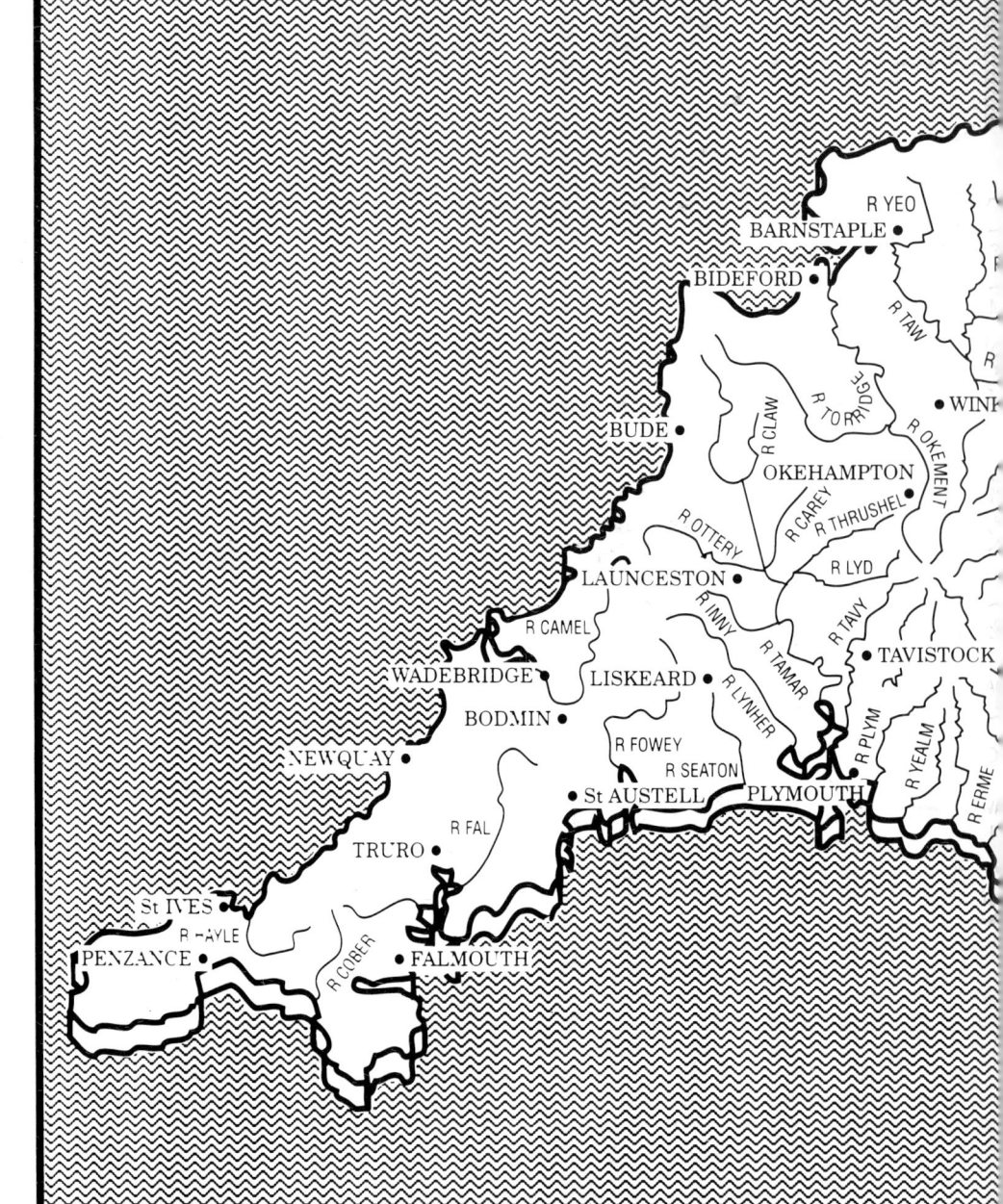